For my daughter, Clara, in the hope that she
will grow up into a world genuinely at peace

MORNINGSIDE
MATA HARIS

HOW MI6 DECEIVED SCOTLAND'S GREAT AND GOOD

———

DOUGLAS MACLEOD

Birlinn

First published in 2005 by
Birlinn Limited
West Newington House
10 Newington Road
Edinburgh EH9 1QS

www.birlinn.co.uk

ISBN10: 1 84341 021 4
ISBN13: 978 1 84341 021 8

British Library Cataloguing-in-Publication Data
A catalogue record for this book is available from the British Library

Typeset by Hewer Text, Edinburgh
Printed and bound by Antony Rowe Ltd, Chippenham

Contents

List of Plates

Acknowledgements

Poles are fond of what they claim to be old sayings, many of which are not in fact all that old. One such saying is 'He who says it takes two to tango, forgets the band.' A writer's band is rather a large one. First off there are those who catalogue, tend and fetch in archives and libraries. My thanks are due to the staff of the National Archive at Kew and the National Library of Scotland in Edinburgh for their knowledge, helpfulness and efficiency; in both organisations the words 'public service' still have real meaning. Also helpful beyond the call of duty was the charming Jane Anderson, in charge of the archive at the Atholl Estates in Perthshire. Every writer needs luck, and luck came in the shape of Tully Jackson, a Haddington historian, who had photographs of the SS Galizien Division in the local refugee camp in the late 1940s.

A part of this story has been made into a radio programme for BBC Scotland, and the producer is Amanda Hargreaves. Amanda and I have worked on a number of projects together and my public acknowledgement of her patience, intelligence and good humour is long overdue. Thanks are also due, on this part of the enterprise, to Carole Purcell, the programme's PA.

All writers need people to bounce ideas off, and all journalists setting out to write books need people to hassle them. My colleague Peter Aitchison filled both roles admirably and also provided the initial impetus to set me off on the long journey of writing a book. Three other colleagues fulfilled the role of patient listeners whose eyes did not visibly glaze over when I launched into some monologue regarding the book: Anne Brown, Heather Fraser and Colin Mackay. It must be said of Heather and Colin, however, that they are well practised at the art of defying visible signs of boredom, as their professional lives are dominated by covering the day-to-day deliberations of the Scottish Parliament. Kim Philby's biographer, Philip Knightley, was unstinting in his help, as was Stephen Dorrill, historian and writer on the British Security Services. Professor Chris Harvie of Tübingen University was, as always, on hand for discussion and advice. My thanks also to my editor at Birlinn, Michèle le Roux, for her meticulous attention to detail.

Finally, there is the writer's long-suffering family, who not only had to suffer the monologues over breakfast, but also bulging files and groaning bookcases cluttering up their lives. My partner, Helen Ross, not only put up with all of that; she also, thankfully, did the proof reading.

Chapter One

Death in the Forest

A heatwave returned to Edinburgh on 12 June 1950: ice cream vendors set out stalls in Princes Street Gardens, sharp-suited boys lay on the grass below the castle with flouncy-skirted girls and chanced their luck, at Portobello the fun fairs raked in the profits. In Central Hall delegates to the Convention of Resistance Movements in Europe and Asia sweltered as the temperature climbed to seventy-five degrees Fahrenheit, and speakers raged against the Soviet Union and 'the enslavement of small nations by Bolshevism and the new Russian imperialism'.

The meeting, organised under the banner of the Scottish League for European Freedom, attracted the good and the great of Edinburgh. Morningside matrons had laboured long and hard at sales of work, coffee mornings and beetle drives to raise cash for the event. They now listened to exotic men from exotic places with strange and unfamiliar names – Turkestan, Idel-Ural, Caucasia and the Ukraine – men passionately pleading their case for freedom. However, to those in the know, they were, in the words of one Foreign Office official, 'the usual number one Nazi beasts'. Men like the Hungarian, General Colonel Ferenc Farkas, a man who had headed a special court which had ordered the execution of opponents of

1

the pro-Nazi wartime government in Budapest; or Yaroslav Stetzko, who had seen service in the cause of the Third Reich at Lviv.

They performed under the sly eye of the League's chairman, John Finlay Stewart. A man approaching his eightieth year, silver haired and still wiry, still a charmer with women of a certain age, still a 'fine figure of a man' in his hunting Stewart kilt, he was a one-time engineer, forestry expert, and still, essentially what he had always really been – a spy. This was a lavish production, a far more costly enterprise than could have been paid for by the efforts of the good and great with tea urns, coffee pots and tombola stalls. It was, in fact, funded by MI6, who had organised passports and paid the travelling and hotel expenses. What was seen by the citizens of Edinburgh as a campaigning charity to help refugees from eastern Europe was in reality no such thing. It was a talent-spotting operation by MI6, whose plan was to set up spy rings amongst the ethnic minorities of the Soviet Union, and foment the internal de-stabilisation of the USSR.

Edinburgh's weather can have a somewhat Presbyterian flavour in early summer, in that you pay for a good day with a chill evening haar rolling in from the North Sea, and 12 June 1950 was no exception. As the fog descended on the city, members of the Galizien Division of the SS held a reunion in the North British Hotel. It is likely, as was their custom on these regimental occasions, that uniforms were worn.

The Scottish League and its sister organisation, the British League for European Freedom, arose out of the friendship and common cause of two remarkable women, Katherine 'Kitty' Murray, Duchess of Atholl, and Elma Dangerfield, journalist and one-time intelligence officer. Kitty was a prominent Westminster politician who, as a testimony to the polarisation of politics in the 1930s, managed to be condemned by the right as the 'Red Duchess', and by the left as the 'Fascist Beast'. In fact she was a one-nation Tory of the rural Scottish variety, with a passionate hatred of the totalitarianism of both right and left which had fashionable support amongst great swathes of the British intelligentsia and chattering classes in that grim decade.

Dangerfield is, however, more complex. A slight, red-haired woman of fierce intellect with a penchant for Byron and for cats, and a liking for gin that persisted into her nineties, she was the widow of a naval officer killed in combat. Early in the war she served in MI9, that branch of the security services heavily parodied in the Bond films, where they made gadgets. These were not, of course, rocket-firing sports cars, but more prosaic objects: wafer-thin maps that could be concealed in fountain pens; miniature compasses the size of finger nails – devices and aids for POWs which could be smuggled into the camps in the mail. She then moved to the Admiralty, and, when I met her in 2003, she was interestingly vague about her time there. Seeking to do more for the war effort, she was encouraged by Duff Cooper at the Ministry of Information to turn to journalism and to take an interest in east European émigrés.

She became close to the Polish government in exile and took an unfashionable interest in what became one of the longest-running and, certainly post-Second World War, one of the most pointless cover-ups in Foreign Office history, the truth about who carried out the Katyn massacre. In 1939 Poland had been carved up by Nazi Germany and the USSR.

At fifteen minutes past four o'clock on the morning of 22 June 1941, however, the German invasion of the Soviet Union was launched and the Red Army became our gallant allies. The murderous Joseph Stalin, dictator of all the Russias, was spun into the avuncular figure of 'Uncle Joe'. Events in eastern Poland between 1939 and 1941 were, in the corridors of Whitehall power, best ignored in the interests of the war effort. The truth about Katyn would not sit easily with visions of our new, glorious Soviet ally. 'My enemy's enemy is my friend' was a dictum designed to be a spectre at future feasts.

Katyn is a primeval Russian forest, mostly coniferous, with scattered hardwoods and scrub. There is a hill, known locally as 'Kozinaya Gora', the Hill of the Goats. A mile away there is an inconsequential railway station, Gniezdovo. There is a Russian saying: 'Bad news comes by train.'

The month of April normally brings spring to this part of the country, and by May the trees are green, but the winter of 1939–40 had been the hardest on record and when the cattle trucks began arriving on 8 April there was still snow in deep shade, and mud on the rough road from the station to the Hill of Goats. The trains disgorged their cargo into a barbed-wire cage surrounded by a hardened force of Red Army soldiers. They brought not cattle, but the cream of the Polish army. From the cage they were taken in trucks up the rough road to the Hill of Goats. They came in a steady stream; some six or seven thousand Polish officers made the one-way journey. When they reached the hill their hands were bound. If a man struggled, his greatcoat was thrown over his head, tied round his neck, and he was led, hooded, to the edge of a pit. Those who went quietly to their death stared for a moment into the pit, where the bodies of those who had come before lay, packed head to feet, like sardines. Then they were shot in the base of the skull.

Even as they trundled up the rough road many of those men would have known that some terror lay at journey's end. The Polish officer class were an educated elite, and the historians amongst them would have known that Katyn was the place where the Bolsheviks had killed an unknown number of Tzarist officers in 1919.

When the Red Army had finished shooting Poles in the back of the neck, they filled in the pits, smoothed the clods, and planted conifers. It was late in the season to be planting young trees, but they chose well, for when, three years later, another army came to the forest – the Wehrmacht – the sap was beginning to run in the young Scots pines. They had heard the rumours and, in the far milder spring of 1943, exhumed the mass graves.

In Berlin the propaganda minister, Joseph Goebbels, was ecstatic. In terms of spin the news couldn't have come at a better time. Since 1942 the British and Soviet media had been running accurate accounts of Nazi deportations and escalating mass murder. Even the BBC, who had on one occasion issued a memo following a broadcast about the extermination of the Jews warning of the dangers 'of giving these people an inch lest they take a mile', was reporting on the final solution. Goebbels was directing his propaganda machine to portray the Soviet Union as a 'pestilential world enemy'. As the war in the east turned against the Third Reich, German propaganda was increasingly aimed at occupied western Europe, seeking to turn the conflict in the popular imagination into a defence of European civilisation and culture against a barbarian threat from the east. Its purpose was to raise non-German units for the attrition on the Eastern Front.

The report from an SS Unterscharführer on a mass grave at Katyn was, therefore, a gift to Goebbels. The officer reported that 'numerous identification papers, dogtags, amulets and diaries' had been recovered and that 'none of the dated material is later than 1940'. The Nazis flew journalists and delegates from neutral countries and the occupied West to the site, along with reporters, academics, and priests from Poland itself. What they saw in the forest and how it was reported struck Goebbels as so horrifying it would become a 'huge political issue' which would drive a wedge between the West and the Soviets.

The Nazis initially announced the discovery of the mass grave on 12 April 1943 on the radio station, Donausender. The initial reaction of the Foreign Office was an understandable caution that this 'terrible accusation may be another lie put out by German propaganda in order to spoil Polish–Soviet relations . . . and to wipe out in the opinion of the world the impression created by recent revelations of German atrocities.'

Within weeks, however, the truth was spelt out to Whitehall in a report from the British Ambassador to the Polish government in exile, Owen O'Malley. It boiled down to simple and terrible mathematics, allied to growing eye-witness accounts from Poles who had escaped Soviet clutches and made often epic journeys to the west to continue the struggle against Nazism. In 1939 the Red Army captured between nine and ten thousand Polish officers. Nothing had been heard of them since 1940. At the beginning of 1940 they were in three prison camps, at Kozielsk, Starobielsk and Ostashkov. In March

1940 they were told that by personal order of Comrade Stalin himself they were to be moved to 'more agreeable' conditions, and they 'might look forward to eventual release'. Before the journey they were inoculated, fresh finger prints were taken, Polish documents which had been confiscated were returned, they were given rations for the journey, and more senior officers were given sandwiches wrapped in clean white paper, a commodity seldom seen anywhere in the Soviet Union.

According to O'Malley's report: 'Entrainment of the officers from the three camps went on all through April and the first half of May, and the lorries, lined with cheerful faces, which took them from camp to station, were, in fact, the last that was ever seen of them alive by any witness to which we have access . . . Only the testimony of scribblings on the railway wagons in which they were transported affords any indication of their destination. The same wagons seem to have done a shuttle service between Kozielsk and the detraining station and on these some of the first parties had scratched the words, "Don't believe that we are going home", and the news that their destination had turned out to be a small station near Smolensk.'

Not all the captured Polish officers were murdered in Katyn. An unknown number were taken to 'northern islands' and loaded onto three barges which were towed out into the Arctic Ocean and sunk.

All of this, and, as time passed, even more detailed accounts, were known to the Foreign Office and suppressed for decades. The British government 'held aloof' from a cynical attempt by the Russians to pin the massacre on the Nazis at the Nuremburg trials. Between 1950 and 1952, in the United States, a Congressional enquiry was 'not well received' by Whitehall mandarins, with 'its predictable verdict of Soviet guilt'. Two conflicting reports in the 1950s are appended with an FO official's note that 'this muddies the water beautifully'. By 1970 the aim was still suppression although by this time it had become nearly impossible, 'increasingly strained by the accumulation of pointers to Soviet responsibility'. However, the conclusion remained that 'despite public pressure there is no evident advantage in departing from the policy in disclaiming British standing in the murder and disappearance of Polish officers on Soviet territory', or in 'breaking the silence we have preserved for nearly thirty years on the Katyn massacre'. There may well have been good reasons, given the desperate struggle with Nazi Germany in the 1940s, but subsequent suppression seems simply to expose the curiously secretive mind of the Foreign Office civil servant of the time, allied, perhaps, to a lingering anti-Polish sentiment.

Almost as fast as the Foreign Office were trying to conceal what they knew, the Polish government in exile were leaking it. Given that the sources were primarily Polish, it seems remarkable that Whitehall mandarins thought they would do anything other than leak it. The Poles issued an official public communiqué. They said they understood that the Nazis were masters of the big lie, but it remained a fact that thousands of Poles had been captured by the Soviet Union and all enquiries as to their fate had met with silence from the Kremlin. Letters to relatives and loved ones from the POWs in Soviet hands had suddenly stopped in the spring of 1940. They had asked, the statement said, for the Red Cross to dispatch a commission to investigate the Katyn massacre. By an unfortunate coincidence they chose the very day Berlin made the same request, thus allowing *Pravda* to simply accuse the Poles

8

of working hand in glove with the Nazis. On 26 April Molotov broke off relations with the 'bourgeois London Polish government'.

All Stalin ever said when questioned about the missing officers was, 'they escaped to Manchuria', or just, with an avuncular smile and a shrug, 'things sometimes happen'. Goebbels rejoiced, writing in his diary on 28 April: 'The break is seen as a complete triumph for German propaganda, especially for me personally . . . All of a sudden fissures are appearing within the allied camp.' The British Foreign Office orchestrated a propaganda campaign in the press, portraying the Poles as 'irresponsible' and as conducting a 'private war on Russia'.

As the spring of 1943 bloomed into early summer a delegation from the Polish government in exile visited Elma Dangerfield's elegant Chelsea home. They brought a vodka made from morello cherries, traditionally a drink for ladies. She found it a tad sweet, but better than nothing in those rationed times. She was later to find starka, a vodka made from bison grass, more to her taste. The purpose of their visit was to deliver into her hands a dossier on the Katyn massacre and other atrocities committed by the Soviet Union in eastern Poland between 1939 and 1941.

Dangerfield had found an outlet for her journalism in *The Nineteenth Century and After*, an influential journal which mingled politics and foreign affairs with literary, intellectual and poetic pieces. For this lover of romantic poets in general, and Byron in particular, the curious mix gave her, along with journalistic opportunities, the chance to indulge her own poetic efforts, poems such as 'The Ghost', which ends:

Have you ever met a ghost in the terrible still night?
With a face as passionless as the cold starlight
Stumbling through the universe and straining to the sky?
I have met that ghost – and that ghost was I.

The magazine's editor, F.A. Voigt, was one of those legions of journalists who duck and weave in and out of that rough trade and in and out of the rougher trade of intelligence. It is something of an English tradition, dating at least as far back as Daniel Defoe, who spied on the Scots in the run-up to Union. Frederick Augustus Voigt was born in Hampstead in 1892, his donnish bespectacled look belying considerable physical and intellectual courage. Christened Fritz, he preferred the anglicised Frederick, Freddy to his friends and fellow journalists. He achieved first class honours at Birkbeck College, and taught himself Latin, Greek and Anglo-Saxon. He served for four years in the artillery during the First World War and joined the *Manchester Guardian* in 1920. After a spell in the advertising department he was sent to Berlin as assistant to the paper's correspondent there, J.G. Hamilton, whom he coached in German. Hamilton was soon posted to the, for him, more congenial surroundings of Paris, and Voigt became the *Manchester Guardian*'s Berlin correspondent, a job he held for more than ten years.

Those were the hollow years for Germany, the years of the great inflation, of Weimar and its fledgling yet flawed democracy, ultimately impotent and decadent, besieged by menace from both left and right. Yet Berlin became a capital of avant-garde art, experimental music, theatre and writing. It also became, in the eyes of the essentially conservative Germany beyond the city boundaries, a byword for sleaze, a 'modern Sodom'. If this was the city's age of Bauhaus, it was also its age of 'Cabaret'. On the Kurfurstendamm the red-booted prostitutes strutted their stuff under the candelabra street lights; in sleazy jazz clubs George Grosz figures, obese and slavering profiteers, pawed half-starved girls and sniffed cocaine; the high heels of transvestite hookers clicked along a Friedrichstrasse gaudy with neon and lined with gay bars, clip joints and clubs pandering to every perversion and fetish known to humanity. To the gloomy German philosopher Oswald Spengler, a hero of Nazi intellectuals, though no Nazi himself, Weimar was not a fledgling democracy but a 'dictatorship of party bosses . . . erected in smiling comfort over the corpses of two million heroes who died in vain, over a nation which withered away in misery'. Joseph Goebbels was uncharacteristically more succinct. To him it was 'a dung heap'.

Voigt observed at first hand the polarisation of German politics into two anti-democratic camps – Communist and National Socialist – and the failure of a democracy in which the people had lost faith. In a nation demoralised by defeat, whose economy was all but destroyed by inflation and reparations, ill-equipped to deal with the ice storm of the Great Depression, much political life was conducted by the fist and the club on the streets. Voigt showed great courage in reporting this dangerous chaos. A fellow journalist wrote of him that 'he would rather be burned at the stake than frightened off a story'. On one occasion he was investigating the influence of the extreme right on the German army when he was kidnapped, and, bound and blindfolded, the wall to either side of him was sprayed with bullets. When Hitler came to power and created, in Voigt's words, 'the bloodshot darkness of the Third

11

Reich', he had to flee Berlin, pursued by the Gestapo, for Paris, and from 1934 until 1940 he was diplomatic correspondent of the *Manchester Guardian*.

He was also working for MI6, using his cover as part of the Z-network of spies, designed to penetrate Germany from bases in Switzerland. It was operated by Colonel Claude Dansey, who ran it almost as if it were an independent intelligence unit. According to Kim Philby, he was 'an elderly gentleman of austerely limited outlook' who, quite bizarrely for an Assistant Chief of the Secret Service, 'regarded counter espionage as a waste of effort in wartime'. He also seems to have been something of a bully, 'whose speciality was the barbed little minute, which creates the maximum of resentment to no obvious purpose'.

Voigt's involvement did not end there. With Edward Hulton, publisher of *Picture Post*, he set up a news agency, Britanova, which was a front for the use of MI6 and the dissemination of propaganda. He was involved with Dangerfield in organising the Middle Zone Association, whose philosophy of central European federation was to form the foundation of both the Scottish and British Leagues' propagandising position. These federal ideas were not merely the stuff of intellectual speculation by a few journalists, academics and political thinkers over a few drinks at the club.

In 1943 members of the SS put out feelers for peace. Dansey's chief lieutenant in Berne was Frederick Heuvel, a director of Eno's Fruit Salts, and a papal count. In February a meeting took place at which Heuvel and Alan Dulles, Berne station chief for the US Office of Strategic Services, met a representative of the international department of the SS, one Walter Schellenberg. According to Stephen Dorril, the historian of MI6, Dulles is alleged to have said that the peace should permit the existence of a Greater Federal Germany, which 'would be part of a cordon sanitaire against Bolshevism and Pan Slavism which, in association with a Danubian Federation, would be the best guarantee of order and progress in Central and Eastern Europe'. In short, the Voigt/Dangerfield axis was promoting a developing world view within MI6 and the US security services, a world view, it must be stressed, discussed behind closed doors, both in Britain and on the other side of the Atlantic.

In researching Britain's secret services, the nature of the beast often makes what remains closed as telling as what is opened to the public gaze. Files on Voigt and Britanova's activities in the 1940s, particularly in Turkey, remain firmly shut, as does a file on Voigt and the Middle Zone Association. One can perhaps appreciate that, even after more than forty years, espionage activities in Turkey may still cause a certain frisson of disquiet in that sensitive region, but quite why the Association's file remains closed is something of a mystery best left to conspiracy theorists. Thinking, even MI6 thinking, on eastern Europe in the period between 1942 and 1945 is unlikely to cause any tremors in the current conduct of affairs.

Whatever the undercurrents, it must be said that Dangerfield's journalistic effort on behalf of the Poles was a brave and morally just campaign. It flew in the face of government propaganda portraying the Red Army as heroic and gallant allies. It also flew in the face of public opinion, partly moulded by this propaganda but also containing, on the left, a sentimental attachment to the USSR, a view that, whatever its faults and mistakes, it was essentially a blueprint for 'the future'.

In 1945, when the Red Army had been raping and pillaging its way across eastern Europe, the left-wing magazine *Tribune* carried a report from its Vienna correspondent on the appalling conditions in the city under Soviet occupation. It described the 'monstrous' behaviour of Russian troops, who had raped 100,000 women. Readers protested in the letters column about 'this slander' on the Red Army: some accused the correspondent of lying, but others, with Orwellian doublethink, implied that, even if it was all true, it shouldn't be exposed because of the effect on relations with the USSR, which would give succour to the enemies of 'progressive' opinion.

In a piece attacking this point of view George Orwell made an astonishing admission, which illustrates the degree to which Whitehall strove to maintain the mythology of alliance: 'I have had writings of my own kept out of print because it was feared that the Russians would not like them.' Dangerfield, it seems, experienced no such restraints. In an article, 'Deportees', published in *The Nineteenth Century and After* in 1943, she went beyond the truth about the Katyn massacre to examine the treatment of ordinary Poles during the Soviet occupation between 1939 and 1941. 'One million Poles,' she wrote, 'about half of them women and children, were deported by the Russians after the occupation of eastern Poland by the Red Army.'

She told the story of a family who lived near Lemberg. Russian soldiers swarmed through their farm, removed all livestock, cattle and produce, and took all the shared implements from the estate. Deprived of their livelihood the family took refuge in the city itself, where they 'lived in daily dread of deportation'.

Death in the Forest

Come spring, some friends, branded by the Soviet authorities as 'intellectuals' (a favourite target of Stalin), disappeared. Then, one April midnight, the knock came at the door. The members of the Soviet secret police, then known as the NKVD, checked them against a list, ordered them out of the house with what belongings they could carry, and marched them to the railway station. The ubiquitous cattle trucks of the holocaust were waiting, 'the sanitary arrangements consisting of a hole in the floor, and the only light and ventilation coming through two small windows high up in the roof'. The guards shouted in Russian that they were 'Polish bourgeois scum', and their dogs growled. The doors slid shut and darkness fell within the trucks. The trucks were sealed, as the great metal bars slammed home with a final-sounding thud into their brackets. The huge Soviet engine exhaled steam, blew its whistle, and rolled east with its cargo of 1,000 Poles. For four days they had no food or water. When, at last, they were allowed out they drank from a pool, 'ravenously, like animals'. After that, two of them were allowed out once a day to fetch a small amount of bread and water, which was 'quite insufficient for the number of people in the truck'. For eighteen days they trundled across the steppes, through the forests, into the often pathless wastes of Khazakhstan, where, at a nameless halt, the train stopped, the sealed trucks were opened and the deportees were told to get out.

'They were then piled one on top of the other in motor cars which drove them over mud-flooded roads for twenty-four hours into the mountains. There they were ejected and told to live as best they could. When they asked where and how, the Russian guard said, "that is your concern".'

15

Others, cited by Dangerfield, were sent to labour camps in the Siberian forests. 'They lived in barracks with the foresters and other Polish and Russian exiles, some of whom had been there for ten years.' Families were separated, husbands from wives, children from parents, and for the pious Poles 'the lack of all religious comfort appears to have caused even greater mental anguish than the sheer physical discomforts and malnutrition'. The death rate was colossal, and Dangerfield's estimate of between two and three hundred thousand may even be on the low side. 'Information shows', she wrote, 'that the mortality was greatest amongst the children who were deported to the Urals, where the climate was most severe; arctic cold in winter, and tropical heat in the summer.' The Soviet authorities did not regard pulmonary infections or chronic rheumatism as legitimate reasons for not working, and the camps were run with the slogan 'those who cannot work, should not eat', as holy Communist writ.

A body of anecdotal evidence about Poland's holocaust at the hands of the Soviets was also growing. Following the Nazi invasion of the USSR, thousands of fit young Polish men incarcerated by the Kremlin in POW camps voted with their feet and walked thousands of miles to join Free Polish forces under London control, rather than throw in their lot with the Russians and fight the now common enemy. Julian Rybarczyk, a former Glasgow businessman, recalled that after defeat by the Nazis his unit decided it was better to surrender to 'fellow Slavs' in the shape of the Red Army than give themselves up to the 'old German enemy'. They were rounded up, herded into cattle trucks, and sent east. They were then dumped in some nameless place in the steppes of central Asia, and told to fend for themselves. The local peasants were told that the Polish soldiers were 'fascists', and 'the enemies of Comrade Stalin and the Soviet Union'. Come the Soviet nemesis and the Nazi invasion the survivors chose to trek almost a thousand miles to join comrades in the west rather than stay and fight alongside the Red Army.

This was in spite of an amnesty and the formation of a Polish army under Moscow command, led by Colonel – soon General – Zygmunt Berling, and 'guided' politically by the Union of Polish Patriots (ZPP), a grouping of pro-Soviet Poles led by Wanda Wasilewsk, a woman of ferocious Stalinist predilections and a countenance which seemed cast in Stalinist concrete.

Dangerfield also wrote one of the first detailed accounts of the Nazi 'final solution', and the rising in the Warsaw ghetto. It was almost as unwelcome in the Foreign Office as her revelations about the Red Army. It would be easy to characterise the FO of the time as, in modern parlance, institutionally antisemitic. As we shall see later, there is an element of truth in this accusation, compounded by a rather large clutch of public school pro-Arab sentimentalists who had always found haven in the Foreign Service. Yet there are more complex motives at play here. There was a genuine desire not to get trapped into running atrocity stories that smacked of the kind used in the First World War – stories which could prove unsustainable and risible. It is ironic that on this occasion the atrocities were on such a scale that even the most inventive propagandist couldn't have made them up. As the initial intelligence came in on what the Nazis were doing in eastern Europe there was a kind of open-mouthed disbelief on the part of many officials. They could understand persecution, mass execution, even the destruction of whole villages, but the idea that the Nazis were exterminating an entire race using industrial methods stretched credibility. They were looking at something entirely new.

There is an intelligence report from 1942 which illustrates the point. It is not about extermination – quite the reverse. It concerns a camp near Lodz for 'the improvement of the Nordic Race'. According to the agent: 'Every hut in the camp was occupied by a youthful couple, a German boy and a Polish girl or a Pole and a German girl. Their days are spent in games, PT, swimming, lectures and group excursions. The food is excellent. In return, their duty is to engage in sexual intercourse . . . Girls found pregnant are sent to Germany.' An official has appended a note to this report that, 'after giving birth it is easy to guess at the fate of the girl, at best work on the land, at worst, women for the army.' This is, of course, quite wrong. The truth was far more terrifying. The girl would be an honoured mother of the Lebensborn programme, for this was the selective breeding of human beings. The girl would become like a prize mare, impregnated by the prize stallions of the SS, something altogether more alien, a leap into a frightening future.

Poland was being 'Germanised'. Racial scientists scoured the country for those who could be deemed Aryan, some of whom were sent to the breeding camps, others settled on farms and in properties from which ethnic Poles had been expelled. The whole of northern and western Poland was annexed by the Reich. The Polish inhabitants were to be removed and replaced by Germans. The dumping ground was the so-called General Government, described by Neil Ascherson as 'a native reserve under martial law to be

18

exploited for its resources and labour without consideration for the consequences.'

The Jews were to be exterminated. In her 'Battle of the Ghetto', published in October 1943, Dangerfield gave a classic account of the Treblinka death camp, of the cattle trucks disgorging their human cargo from the Warsaw Ghetto, of the illusion all was well, with posters declaring, 'Do not worry about your fate. You are all going to the east to work. You should deposit your valuables here. You will get a receipt, and after you have had your bath and been deloused you will get everything back.'

'After they have been stripped,' she wrote, 'the farce ends, and they are driven along a pathway about 200 metres under the whips of the SS guards towards a strange-looking one-storeyed brick barrack which still has an unfinished appearance. They are greeted at the door by Sauer, the Chief, who drives them with a cat-of-nine tails into a corridor 9 feet wide with 5 chambers on either side.'

The piece was clearly written from intelligence gathered from local Poles, and up to this point is an entirely accurate description of Treblinka. Regarding what happened in the gas chambers and beyond, details are sketchy. Dangerfield could not know that the Jews were gassed with Zyklon B, rather than, as she thought, scalded to death with steam. Nor could she know about the ovens and the industrial disposal of the corpses.

In the 1930s there were many people who were parlour-room advocates of eugenics, who talked blithely about 'eliminating the unfit' from society, 'improving the stock' and of a 'Jewish Question'. They were now reading reports of their easy words made terrible flesh in Poland. It is easy to think of the mandarins of the Foreign Office as being somehow far removed from public opinion, which is, I think, a little unfair. Orwell in 'Notes on Nationalism' explored the ambiguities of British reaction to the unfolding horrors: 'For quite some six years the British admirers of Hitler contrived not to learn of the existence of Dachau and Buchenwald. And those who are loudest in denouncing the German concentration camps are often quite unaware, or only very dimly aware, that there are also concentration camps in Russia. Huge events like the Ukrainian famine of 1933, involving the deaths of millions of people, have actually escaped the attention of the majority of English Russophiles. Many British people have heard almost nothing about the extermination of German and Polish Jews during the present war. Their own antisemitism has caused a vast crime to bounce off their consciousness.'

Dangerfield had been even-handed in exposing both Soviet and Nazi war crimes, and could certainly never have been accused of not publishing a piece because it would have offended the Russians. For her pains she was now persona non grata at the Foreign Office. This was, of course, far from being persona non grata at MI6. Her next venture was to purchase, with the 'assistance of some Polish money', *The Whitehall News*, an influential foreign affairs magazine. The tide of war had turned and minds were being concentrated on the shape of peacetime Europe, a shape in which the prospect of a Soviet Empire loomed darkly. The magazine became a vehicle for the ideas being espoused and expanded by the Middle Zone Association and her friend and MI6 confidant, F.A. Voigt. It also became a conduit for placing in the public domain intelligence on what was happening in the

Soviet Union and eastern Europe. Dangerfield brought on board the charismatic and forceful Scotswoman with strong views on the evils of Communism, Fascism and Nazism: Katherine Murray.

Chapter Two

Fascist Beast: Red Duchess

History has been unkind to Katherine 'Kitty' Murray, Duchess of Atholl. Scotland's first female member of parliament, and the Tory party's first woman minister, just does not fit into modern Scottish iconography.

The Tories have never forgiven her for resigning the whip in 1938 and fighting her seat as an independent, in spite of the fact that her stance on the issues over which she chose to fight are resoundingly endorsed by hindsight. Kitty resigned because she believed that the tacit support of the Chamberlain government for Franco in the Spanish Civil War was wrong, that the policy of appeasement was morally corrupt and doomed to failure, and that the threat posed by Hitler was such that Britain must build up its armed forces, particularly the Royal Air Force, post-haste. In his semi-official history, *The Scottish Tory Party*, Gerald Warner dismisses her stand on Spain as amounting to 'asking a Tory government to abandon neutrality in favour of the atheistic Spanish republic'. There is no mention of her support for Churchill and the ending of appeasement, and scant reference to her work as an education minister or her long campaign to expose Soviet slave labour.

Her complexities also prevent feminists from admitting her

to the sisterhood. Before the First World War she spoke on a platform in Glasgow against female suffrage, although she later admitted this was done as a favour to a family friend, and it was something she looked back on in later life with her wry, self-deprecating sense of humour. More importantly, she opposed the Pankhurst scheme for a 'Women's Party', believing politics should not divide along gender lines, although she was always prepared to work with other women, of whatever party, in the House of Commons on specific feminist issues. After a visit to Africa she spoke out against the enforced circumcision of Kikuyu girls, not a subject easily put on the public agenda in the 1920s. As an education minister she was decades ahead of her time, battling to put in place reforms we would nowadays describe as 'child centred'.

Then there is a more general Scottish prejudice against the landed gentry. It is harder for the proverbial camel to pass through the eye of the proverbial needle than for a Scottish aristocrat to pass into the pantheon of national icons. And Kitty most surely belonged to this class. Born in 1874, she was the daughter of Sir James Ramsay, head of an aristocratic family who had been lairds of Bamff, in Perthshire, since 1232. Her father had three daughters by a first marriage. It was a long-vanished world of paternalism, of a class who saw themselves as having a God-given right to administer an Empire on which the sun never set. Her grandparents on her mother's side were killed in the Indian Mutiny and 'only the devotion of a native bearer saved my mother from sharing the fate of her baby brother'.

Yet she was, in a sense, a victim of that structure. A succession of childhood illnesses turned her into a somewhat bookish girl. The great passion and talent of the young Kitty

23

was, however, music. She developed a sound technique on the piano and a burning intellectual desire to understand how music works. In 1887 she was enrolled in the Wimbledon High School for Girls, where she learned harmony, counterpoint and composition. Thus far it may seem she was acquiring the accomplishments expected of any young Victorian lady, but in 1892 she won the piano scholarship to the Royal College of Music. She studied composition under Sir Hubert Parry, largely remembered today for 'Jerusalem', but in his own time a highly regarded composer of orchestral and choral works.

There is a fundamental decency that emerges again and again in Kitty. In her first year at college she met a somewhat dejected 'young coloured student named Coleridge-Taylor'. He told her he could not afford to continue his studies. Kitty reckoned she could pay her own way and handed her scholarship over to him. Samuel Coleridge-Taylor became, against the racial odds in Victorian and Edwardian England, a prolific and commercially successful composer, after making his reputation with a setting of Longfellow's 'Hiawatha's Wedding Feast', still his most popular work.

She developed a taste for the modern and revolutionary music of Richard Wagner, attending the first complete Ring Cycle at Covent Garden in 1893 and declaring that she was 'thrilled by it', so thrilled, in fact, that she trod the sacred Wagnerian path to Bayreuth for the Ring and for *Parsifal*. She also had a cutting-edge taste in theatre. She saw the first performance of Bernard Shaw's *Arms and the Man*, and thought it 'inaugurated quite a new type of theatre'. Kitty took to that engine and symbol of emerging female emancipation, the bicycle, to the consternation of her family.

That consternation grew to epic proportions when it became clear that Kitty had the talent and the will to become a
professional pianist. It was one thing to have a daughter of the
estate who could adorn the the big house with concert-
standard playing at soirées, quite another to have her out
on the road in the bohemian world of artistic salons, wild-eyed
conductors, and dubious impresarios. It was not the done
thing. There was the serious question of finding a suitable
husband.

The family charged a favourite aunt, one Mary Hill Wilson,
to talk Kitty out of turning professional. Wilson told her that
'she feared that [she] should have to concentrate so much on
technique that it would have a narrowing influence on [her]
life'. Kitty respected her aunt: 'she was so fond of music that
her words carried a good deal of weight'. For possibly the last
time in her life Kitty was talked into doing something against
her better judgement. She missed the autumn term at college,
and 'let country house visits alternate with work at home'.

Giving up her career was not quite a done deal, as she
returned to the Royal College of Music in the following spring
term of 1895. There is a sense of her drawing a line under her
dying dream, a final performance of Schumann's *Kreisleriana*,
and the completion of a composition, published the following
year, a setting of 'A Child's Garden of Verses'. As a composer
Kitty was no lost genius, but this is music which is above
average for a student piece. This fundamental grasp of musical
language was allowed to emerge occasionally in future years,
in the few pieces she wrote at her husband's request for the
Highland bagpipe, but the piano lid was finally closed on
hopes of a professional career.

She met her future husband in 1896, and one gets the

impression her family pointed her in the direction of the eldest son of Atholl and crossed their collective fingers in the hope that this 'musical nonsense' would finally cease. Kitty was the first to admit that she was striking rather than beautiful, but she was dark and curvaceous, wore her intellect lightly, and had a self-deprecating wit. She could certainly charm even such connoisseurs of the female gender as Lloyd George and Bernard Shaw. The Ramsays were invited to Atholl Palace. Kitty took a volume of Beethoven quartets and a novel, 'to keep me going if I did not find much in common with the family or other guests'. There was no room for her and her bicycle on the brake that met them at Blair Atholl railway station, so she cycled up to the castle and there met a 'young man in an Atholl tartan kilt and a grey cloth coat', the eldest Atholl son, then the Marquis of Tullibardine, henceforth 'Bardie' to Kitty.

He was a cavalry officer, a romantic figure who had seen action against Islamic fundamentalists in the Middle East, in ruthless and bloody desert skirmishes. He was twice mentioned in dispatches, and was the first Household Cavalry officer to be awarded the DSO. He had expected a 'blue stocking and was somewhat annoyed she had been invited. But seeing Kitty arrive on a bicycle and wearing a bright cerise bow in her hat cheered me up.'

They were smitten, and married in 1899. It must be stressed that this was no mere marriage of aristocratic convenience, two suitable Scottish families joined in matrimony for reasons of land and estates. There is a sense of deep and genuine love between the pair, tinged with a sadness at their failure to have children.

Almost at once Kitty found herself in an unfamiliar role, an officer's wife in time of war in a combat zone. The Boer War marked a turning point in Imperial conflict and contained lessons about the changed nature of warfare which were woefully misunderstood by all the participants, in particular the group of British officers who were the coming men and would be the leaders of 1914. It was not the marksmanship of the Boers or the nature of the terrain that had made it such a hard war; it was the very nature of war itself that had changed.

The change came about as one of the great unintended consequences of science, and was initially the result of an accident in a laboratory. In 1846 Christian Schoenbaum, Professor of Chemistry at Basle University, spilt some sulphuric acid. He wiped it up with cotton wool, which he forgot to dispose of safely. It dried off, and the professor discovered exploding cotton wool, something not as humorous as it sounds. Guncotton made possible a whole range of wonder-weapons. It was three times as powerful as gunpowder, didn't produce soot in the barrel, and was virtually smokeless and flashless.

Once you had guncotton you could shoot further, and were less liable to be spotted; you could rifle artillery, giving you greater accuracy, produce bigger and nastier fragmenting shells, and you could make rapid-firing machine guns. In short, you could kill and maim more people. For the European powers the last gunpowder war was the Crimean; the new weapons that followed had, thus far, been used in the colonial sphere. What happened when both sides were armed with the new ordnance and guns became clear to the Americans during the Civil War – hence the disbelieving general whose last words were, 'They couldn't hit an elephant at this range.' They couldn't have in the age of gunpowder, but now they could.

Hence the appalling casualty rate of that war. In South Africa the German arms giant Krupp supplied the Boers with the new artillery, rifles and Maxim guns.

According to Thomas Pakenham's definitive history of the Boer War there were over one hundred thousand casualties of all kinds among the 365,000 imperial and 83,000 colonial soldiers involved in the conflict. As to the number of Africans who were killed fighting on the British side, nobody was counting. The British army did learn some lessons about the construction of trench systems and the power of rapid fire, but failed to grasp the big lesson – that the balance of power had tilted vastly in favour of defence in any conflict between the industrialised powers. They even failed to learn that in any such war the age of cavalry charges was gone forever.

Into this dress rehearsal in the sun for the First World War stepped Kitty, a young woman whose experience of life thus far had been bookish, intellectual and musical, spiced with the social life of the debutante. The officer's wife was ex-pected, in the phrase of the time, 'to follow the colours'. She did so with courage and style and was not content to mull over tea and scandal with the other spouses. Of the British war dead, sixteen thousand perished of wounds, disease and poor medical care. She was appalled that there was no British Red Cross to look after the welfare of the sick and wounded. She worked in hospitals and organised entertainment for the troops. She gained a reputation as a woman who could get things done.

She brought her new-found organisational skills back to civilian life and Atholl. There was, of course, the work of the future laird's lady: management of the Caledonian Ball, shoots to be arranged, curling matches in the winter, and charities to be supported. She cut her political teeth in the only way then possible for a woman, by proxy, through support for her husband's campaigns. He became the MP for Perth and Kinross in 1907, and a feature of his election campaigns until he gave up the seat in 1917 was Kitty's tours around the scattered constituency, addressing public meetings where she honed her skills in demolishing hecklers. She tolerated no slackers and took to visiting meetings of the Working Men's Unionist Association between elections, 'in the hope of stirring them up to greater activity'.

One specific political battle, and one which will further not endear her to current Scottish sensibilities, was opposition to Liberal proposals for land reform in the shape of a Small Holders Bill, which would have broken up the sporting estates and applied the Crofting Acts to the whole of Scotland. In 1909 Kitty and Bardie invited Liberals from city constituencies to the Atholl estates to see for themselves. Two London lawyers were enjoying a fishing holiday and, whilst lingering over a dram in the Atholl Arms Hotel, were corralled by Kitty and talked into joining the expedition and writing a report on the outcome. At the end of a day trampling over the wilder reaches of the estate, a Dundee Liberal, a supporter of the bill, concluded that what he had seen was so barren that 'it is wholly unsuitable for small holdings, allotments, pendicles or crofts . . . it simply consists of moss, peat, boulders and swamps'. When passed, the bill was rendered impotent by amendments.

Kitty was to call her too-slim autobiography *Working Partnership*, but she was very much the power behind that political partnership. As a cavalry officer Bardie was both resourceful and courageous; as an MP he was plodding but, with her help, a good constituency member, and perceptive on military matters. He warned the government, for example, that assumptions that there would be a six-month warning of a major war were, in the age of railway timetables and telegraphs, a nonsense. Left to his own devices in matters of business and finance, however, he was hopeless.

His perceptive military mind saw the value of aircraft, and in 1907 experiments were carried out in a hollow in the hills above Glen Tilt on an aeroplane design for the British army by a Lieutenant John Dunn. The experiments were a consummate failure. Bardie's disastrous business judgement took over and he formed a company to promote the design. It was not a financial success. Nor was the scheme he invested in after the First World War to build houses from surplus armour-plated steel originally forged for battleships. His Jamaican sugar plantations failed. His greatest financial folly involved Argentinian trams. He was chairman of a company which planned to co-ordinate public transport in Buenos Aires to avoid 'wasteful competition'. The Argentinian government agreed that integrated transport was a good idea, passed a bill, but made it impossible for foreign investors to get at their capital or share in the profits. Bardie's handling of expenses for a nursing home charity led him to contravene the Lottery Act and he was fined £23 at Bow Street Magistrates Court.

In contrast, Kitty's abilities as an organiser were matchless. In the days before universal suffrage women had little political power, but, provided they belonged to the right class, they did have political influence through what in modern parlance might be described as quangos. In 1912 she was invited to join a committee charged with examining medical services in the Highlands and Islands. She confessed to be 'rather shy at first'. That didn't last. They uncovered an appalling scene: there were thirty-two nurses in Argyll, more than in all the other Highland areas put together. In the Fair Isle, thirty families had been without a doctor for seven years. No doctor meant no vaccinations, and contact with the mainland could mean contact with smallpox and 'whole families swept away'. A doctor in Glenmoriston told of twenty people in one house dying of TB. The committee's recommendations were, for 1912, radical in the extreme: a central health authority, an Imperial Grant to fund improvements, increased salaries for doctors to attract them to remote areas, a district nursing system, the extension of cottage hospitals, and specialised TB units.

Kitty displayed an ability to think beyond the confines of received wisdom, a refusal to toe a party line, which was to lead her to be misunderstood and condemned by those in the 1930s who inhabited political trenches marked 'left' and 'right' and lobbed slogans like hand grenades at one another. She was a devout Christian, who, late in life, fondly remembered her father singing 'the beautiful collects of the Church of England' in the small church in Alyth when she was a child. Yet on the committee's journey through the Highlands and Islands she was disturbed by the number and wealth of churches, compared to the dreadful state of medical services. 'In Midyell, for example, there were no less than ten [churches], all – or nearly all – Free Presbyterian. And well built and comfortable manses were also in sharp contrast to virtual hovels that provided the doctor with accommodation.'

On a later committee, examining the plight of tinkers – what we would now call travellers – she stood out against the unanimity of her colleagues on one issue. The recommendations ran counter to current thinking: what was proposed was that they should be housed, a job creation scheme put in place, furniture and tools provided out of public funds, and land grants made of between one and three acres. At the time this represented progressive opinion. The recommendation Kitty baulked at concerned alcohol. 'I felt obliged to dissent from the proposal of our male colleagues that drink should be prohibited to any tinker benefiting from the proposed scheme.' She felt the proposal was unworkable, degrading, and would be counter-productive.

So Kitty was a talented upper-class woman doing good works and influencing political policy. What changed all that and made possible political power, rather than simply influence, for women was, of course, the First World War. The European powers turned their modern weapons on each other, killing millions, destroying empires, ending dynasties, and bringing down the pit-props of the old order.

It was during this war that the old duke died and Bardie inherited the title. Now Duchess of Atholl, Kitty turned the north wing of the castle into a hospital. She also did battle with Highland landlords who were reluctant to help with the growing food crisis created by an escalating U-boat offensive. A Venison Supply Committee urged the killing of as many deer as possible, and the netting of fresh-water fish to increase available protein. The Atholls promoted these schemes in spite of opposition from a number of fellow estate-owners. The problems created by the U-boats were exacerbated by a labour shortage on the land, particularly acute in the Highlands, with its long tradition of military service. The duchess formed a

Women's Patriotic Committee to enrol female labour on the farms, an idea which was taken up more formally during the Second World War with the formation of the Land Army.

One of the great changes wrought by the war was a Reform Bill extending the electoral base and giving women the right to vote and to become members of parliament, though at first it applied only to females over thirty. It was no less a person than Lloyd George, then prime minister and a Liberal to boot, who first suggested a future in parliament to this formidable Tory woman. Kitty had talked the PM into visiting Atholl, and had demonstrated to him first hand how 'his dream of turning sporting estates into smallholdings was a climatic and geographical impossibility'. Thus it was that in the hills above Glen Tilt, Lloyd George, astride a Highland pony, convinced the duchess to seek out a constituency, telling her: 'You should be failing in your duty to other women if you do not come forward.' In the event, she won Kinross and West Perthshire in the 1923 election by 150 votes, delivering to Scotland its first woman MP.

She had not, thus far, shown any great interest in the politics of eastern Europe, bar one totally bizarre incident in 1920. The Atholls had travelled to Florence for a holiday. It was not an auspicious time to be vacationing in Italy. On the one hand there were strikes, riots and agrarian disturbances, and a sense that the nation was on the verge of its own Bolshevik revolution. On the other hand, Mussolini's Fascist movement was embarked on a campaign of counter-revolutionary terror with the active backing of industrialists and landowners. A ball the Atholls were to attend was cancelled on account of a bomb outrage.

They were approached by a Major Barnes, who had been involved with a hydro-electric plan for Atholl forest. At the very least, it seems Barnes was operating on the fringes of British Intelligence. He was involved in dubious operations in Albania, which had achieved independence from the Turks in 1912. The so-called Great Powers undertook to provide them with a king and settled on a nephew of the Kaiser, Prince William of Wied. It proved a poisoned chalice. He arrived in his new kingdom in the spring of 1914, and within six months these Great Powers were at war with one another. To this day Albania has a decided tendency towards anarchy, with its war lords, tribal rivalries and blood feuds. The First World War predictably tipped the nation into a bout of this anarchy, compounded by foreign intrigue and aggression. William abandoned his throne and fled. Barnes fixed a meeting up between the duke and a group of Albanian leaders in Florence. The Albanians offered Bardie the crown. He refused, but not, it seems, at once. He pondered the matter long enough to canvass the Foreign Secretary, Lord Curzon, who advised him, 'not to take the offer seriously', and long enough to ascertain that the idea 'was also viewed with alarm by Italy'.

Events in the Soviet Union first impinged on the duchess in a thoroughly practical manner. The estate they inherited was already plagued with debt, a situation not helped by the duke's penchant for bad investment. Forestry operations in Dunkeld became an important cash earner, but in the early 1930s cheap Soviet timber was dumped on the UK market, making the Atholl operation a poor economic bet. As a politician, the duchess investigated the Soviet timber industry, and the broader story of Stalin's liquidation of the kulaks (a class of peasant who became proprietors of their own farms after 1906 land reforms), the ruthless collectivisation of farming and the subsequent Ukrainian famine.

In her book, *The Truth about Forced Labour in Russia*, she lifted the lid on the unfolding Stalinist terror, actions by the Soviet state which many, perhaps most, of the British intelligentsia either refused to believe or actually felt were justified. The duchess estimated that five million kulaks were deported, chiefly to the timber areas. It is an entirely accurate estimate. Units of the Red Army and the secret police, then called the OGPU, were joined by brigades of fanatical Communists from the cities, fired up with a hatred of the peasants who, they believed, were holding onto their wealth whilst the urban areas went hungry. Even the name 'kulak' was deliberately pejorative – it is a Russian word meaning: 'grasping fist'.

'Entire families,' the duchess wrote, 'were dispatched, families were broken up. Some were left destitute in their villages. None was allowed to keep more than the clothing on his back. The property handed over to the collective farms was valued at over 400 million roubles. In September 1929, there are said to have been six timber convict camps in existence. By the spring of 1931 they numbered nineteen.' Stalin called this, 'constructing Socialism' through the use of prison labour.

In his *Memoirs of a Revolutionary*, V. Serge recalled: 'Trainloads of deported peasants left for the icy north, the forests, the steppes, the deserts. There were whole populations, denuded of everything; the old folk starving to death mid-journey, new-born babies were buried on the banks of the roadside, and each wilderness had its crop of little crosses of boughs or white wood.'

This was indeed class war. In 1934 a trade agreement was being considered by the House of Commons Russian Trade Committee, of which the duchess was a member, but any thoughts she had of protecting the interests of the timber industry and dealing with the Soviets evaporated. She was approached by 'a young man named Malcolm Muggeridge', who brought her 'ghastly descriptions of the famine in the Ukraine which he had seen'.

Muggeridge was yet another journalist who was to turn his hand to espionage, joining MI6 during the Second World War. In 1929 the *Manchester Guardian*'s Moscow correspondent was due to go on leave, and Muggeridge took his place for a few months. In those few months he made a long intellectual journey from Stalinist sympathiser to anti-Communist. It was partly a very personal odyssey, for he was the nephew-in-law of Sidney and Beatrice Webb, the British apologists for Stalin's regime par excellence.

He went with his wife, filled with idealism, intending to stay. They sold off items they considered bourgeois: a dinner jacket, a ball gown, jewellery and books. On the first evening Red Square seemed perfect. The idyll did not last. He saw a peasant vomiting over a piece of sausage and in a kind of road to Damascus experience in reverse, it came to him that the man was starving.

When Muggeridge returned he wrote of his experiences in fictional form in a novel, *Winter in Moscow*, and he wrote of himself: 'The doubt haunted him on the way back to the hotel. He saw hunger everywhere. In the faces that hurried past him, and in the patient queues and in the empty shops, dimly lighted and decorated with red streamers, whose windows contained only busts of Marx, Lenin and Stalin.'

The kulaks had benefited from Lenin's New Economic Policy. They were, obviously, not only the USSR's most enterprising farmers, but also the nation's best farmers and

Stalin had removed them to the labour camps or exterminated them. Little wonder, then, that famine ensued.

In 1933 Muggeridge returned to the USSR, convincing the *Manchester Guardian* to send him to the outlying areas of the Soviet Union. The West had been poorly served by coverage of Soviet excesses. The most prestigious of the Moscow correspondents was Walter Durante of the *New York Times*, strangely an apologist for the regime, who used the phrase, 'you can't have an omelette without breaking eggs', so often that it became a cliché. Durante had been born in 1887 in Liverpool. He became a reporter for *The Times* during the First World War, where he lost a leg in a railway accident, and, whilst in Paris, fell in with Aleister Crowley, the mad practitioner of black magic, who revelled in the title of 'The Beast'. In the French capital and on a couple of visits to Crowley's house at Boleskin on Loch Ness, he partook of his host's idea of fun, namely, orgies disguised as black magic ritual, devil worship and opium smoking.

Durante reported in his paper that there was no famine. 'There is no actual starvation or death from starvation but there is widespread mortality from diseases due to malnutrition,' was his only concession to any suggestion that there may have been a problem, and he ended with his omelette cliché.

Muggeridge produced the first contemporaneous report on the famine by a Western journalist. Perhaps because he was a former believer, he understood an important feature of the mindset: the words and phrases themselves. He began by pointing this out – that it was easy to sit in Moscow and hear officials talk of the need to collectivise agriculture, or root out the parasitic kulaks, all in the name of building Socialism, that it all sounded so easy and so logical, backed up with the endless stream of Kremlin statistics, and that what he had done was to go and find out what was actually happening in the vast hinterland, over one sixth of the world's land surface.

And what he found was the famine: 'Cattle and horses dead; fields neglected; meagre harvest despite moderately good climate conditions; all the grain that was produced taken by the government; now no bread at all, no bread anywhere, nothing much else either, despair and bewilderment. The Ukraine was before the revolution one of the world's great wheat-producing areas and even Communists admit that its population, including poor peasants, enjoyed a tolerably comfortable standard of life; now it would be necessary to go to Arabia to find cultivators in more wretched circumstances.'

This was a major exclusive. Eight million people had died. It was a vast crime against humanity on a par with the Nazi exterminations of the following decade. The *Manchester Guardian* did run his story over three days, 26 to 28 March 1933, yet didn't give it any great prominence. It did coincide with a report from F.A. Voigt on Nazi persecution of the Jews, but there is no doubt – there was certainly no doubt in the mind of Malcolm Muggeridge – that the paper played the story down, and that they did so because in the 1930s the *Guardian* always gave the benefit of the doubt to the USSR.

In briefing the Duchess of Atholl he reinforced her growing conviction that a human tragedy on a huge scale was being enacted in the Soviet Union, and prompted her lingering pro-Ukranian sentiment. The ferocity of the attack on her for this stance from the intellectual left was what led her to be dubbed 'Fascist Beast'.

The credulity and duplicity of these intellectuals was breathtaking. A letter signed by Bernard Shaw and other luminaries of the left, published in the *Manchester Guardian* in March 1933, declared that reports of a famine in the Ukraine were an 'offensive and ridiculous' attempt to portray the condition of workers in the Soviet Union as one of slavery and starvation. Their letter claimed that on their visits to the USSR, 'Everywhere we saw a hopeful and enthusiastic working class . . . developing public works, increasing health services, extending education, achieving the economic independence of women and the security of the child, and – in spite of many previous mistakes which all social experiments involve at first (and which they have never concealed or denied) – setting an example of industry and conduct.'

According to Muggeridge's biographer, Richard Ingrams, the press corps in Moscow had a bet concerning these periodic visitors who were taken on the enchanted tour of model factories, prisons, creches and camps by Intourist guides spouting statistics. The winner of the pot was the one who could circulate the most incredible Stalinist excuse amongst those dewy-eyed political tourists. Muggeridge won. He was asked by the Labour peer, Lord Morley, why there were so many queues in Moscow. Muggeridge told the peer it was because comrade Stalin was concerned about long working hours and devised queues as a means of giving the workers time to themselves.

To be condemned as a Fascist Beast for standing out against the tide of Soviet propaganda being peddled by the self-styled progressives of the world was bad enough, but the duchess found that when she turned her scepticism on Nazi Germany and on the Spanish Civil War, she metamorphosed into the Red Duchess. In 1935 she sat in on a Labour-sponsored meeting addressed by the new Soviet Ambassador, Ivan Maisky. He was a little gnome-like man with a round brown head, and the Labour members were somewhat alarmed to see the statuesque figure of the anti-Soviet duchess bearing down on the seemingly hapless ambassador at the end of the meeting. She had actually met him first at a dinner at Buckingham Palace, where someone with a sense of humour, an agenda of their own, or a total ignorance of politics, had seated them side by side, and, against the odds, they had got on rather well together. What was on Kitty's mind was German rearmament, and Soviet claims, entirely justified, about the rapid expansion of the Luftwaffe and the development of advanced motorised armoured divisions.

The duchess had been approached by an academic, a specialist in German, who had shown her passages in *Mein Kampf*, particularly those relating to ideas about expanding living space, a Greater Germany, and solving the Jewish 'problem'. For the very good reason that much of the book involved plans for chunks of the USSR, *Mein Kampf* was closely studied in the Kremlin, and Maisky agreed with her that the book was explicit in its blueprint for carving the proposed living space out of great swathes of eastern Slavic Europe and the Soviet Union itself.

What she had discovered was that the English language translation of the book was about a third the size of the German original. This might be construed as a blessed relief, given the nature of the Führer's rant, were it not for the fact that the most bellicose passages had either been expunged or watered down. With the backing of the former editor of *The Times*, Wickham Steed, she published authoritative translations of the more alarming passages in *Mein Kampf*.

Within a couple of months Hitler made his first move on the European stage, when German troops entered the demilitarised Rhineland. The German General Staff warned the Führer that the French would react strongly, to which he replied, 'The French won't move an inch.' It was a crucial moment in what Churchill described as 'the horrible, dull, remorseless drift to war', for at this point Nazi Germany simply did not have the military power to go to war. Had the Allies stood firm over the Rhineland they would have called one of the most audacious bluffs in history.

The duchess organised an all-party tour of three countries in eastern Europe – Yugoslavia, Romania and Czechoslovakia – to assess the darkening mood. Her conclusion was justifiably gloomy: 'Half the continent, it seemed to our party, was trembling in the balance between dictatorship and democracy, and to a large extent the issue might depend on whether we supported the democratic forces.'

In supporting democratic forces she spoke out in favour of the Spanish Republic, fighting for its life against the Fascist General Franco, who was receiving support from Mussolini's Italy and from Nazi Germany. She set up an all-party Committee for Spanish Relief, whose purpose was to evacuate children from areas being bombed by the Kondor Legion of the Luftwaffe, who officially weren't in Spain. By the spring of 1937 the committee had several trucks operating in the bombed areas. On a fact-finding mission to Spain she came under shell fire, managed to meet the legendary La Passionara, and, more importantly, ascertained that Italians fighting for Franco were not 'volunteers', but regular soldiers, and that the Luftwaffe were indeed bombing civilian targets. On returning to the UK she was summoned before one of the organisations she supported, the National Citizens Union, and grilled on her involvement with Spanish politics. Here was the Red Duchess smear taking effect, for she was not re-elected to the post of Vice President. It was an omen of things to come.

The horrors of the war were growing. Franco attacked the Basque country, Guernica was bombed, and subsequently became a symbol for airborne terror. The duchess and her all-party committee managed to get the Home Office to agree to allow two thousand Basque children into Britain. As the children were marched down to the ship that was to take them here, they were bombed, eleven were killed and one hundred were too badly injured to make the journey. When the Basque country fell to Franco some of the children were repatriated to their parents. However, they had to exercise the utmost caution. She discovered some of the requests were politically motivated as 'their presence here was hardly a good advertisement for Franco's rule'.

To counter this propaganda she wrote a book, *Spotlight on Spain*, which sold 100,000 copies in its first week. As a polemic it is, on the surface, rather good. It describes graphically the appalling horrors of that war, and the involvement of the Axis powers. In her final chapter, 'What it means to us', she warned of the danger of a Fascist victory in Spain leading to the UK losing control of the Mediterranean and to France facing another hostile border. She accused the Cabinet of behaving as though they wanted Franco to win, and failing to understand that a Fascist victory and loss of command in the Mediterranean would lead to the loss of India.

What she had failed to notice, and it is hardly surprising, was that the Republic was being torn apart by its own factions – Troskyist, Anarchist and Communist – all with arcane subgroups of their own. She had seen the conflict through the eyes of the Communist party, the largest group, essentially the government, and, as a consequence, fell foul of the pen of George Orwell when he reviewed the book for the *New English Weekly*. Orwell had fought in an Anarchist militia on the Republican side. He didn't actually review the book, but wrote a rather good essay on why the rich are attracted to Socialism: 'There is, of course, nothing surprising nowadays in a pro-communist duchess. Nearly all moneyed people who enter the left wing movement follow the Stalinist line as a matter of course . . . the real question is not why moneyed people are Stalinists, but why they enter the left wing movement at all.'

He was posing an interesting question about the wrong duchess; Kitty was far from being either left wing or a Stalinist. And she had written a bestseller supporting the Republic, exposing the duplicity of Nazi Germany and Italy, and criticising government policy, a government which her own Tory Party supported, not to mention the highly practical point that she had saved some two thousand Basque children.

On 25 April 1938 she wrote to the prime minister, making demands she knew he wouldn't meet and effectively resigning the Tory whip. She called for the end of the so-called 'non-intervention' policy regarding the Spanish Civil War, an immediate declaration by Great Britain of opposition to any further aggression in Europe, and an urgent rearmament programme. This did not, of course, mean that she would have to resign as an MP, for she had enjoyed considerable support within her constituency party. She believed that they had given her a more or less free hand on foreign affairs, but there were dark forces ranged against the duchess, and they launched a

43

smear campaign. She was accused of singing 'The Red Flag' in public, of being in the pay of the Soviets, of having introduced as speakers men who had served in the International Brigades and who 'were said all to have been in serious conflict with the forces of the Crown'. The campaign was orchestrated by an official of the neighbouring Conservative Association, one Captain Luttman-Johnson. He was also a member of a number of pro-Nazi organisations, led by the Tory MP for Peebles, Captain Archibald Maule Ramsay, the only British member of parliament to be imprisoned under Defence Regulation 18B, as a security risk.

Chapter Three

Hitler's Scotsmen

In the early 1970s a huge financial scandal engulfed the multi-national Lohnro company and its charismatic boss, 'Tiny' Roland. It prompted the Conservative prime minister of the time, Edward Heath, to describe Roland as 'the unacceptable face of capitalism'. I was watching a news bulletin when the unacceptable face appeared on screen and my companion, a normally mild-mannered man, suddenly said, 'I knew him. He's a Nazi bastard.' My companion, James Anderson, was an executive with Scottish and Newcastle Breweries, and at the beginning of the Second World War had been in the Royal Army Medical Corps stationed at Peebles Hydro, which had been requisitioned for the duration.

According to Anderson – and his account was never challenged by Roland – the future tycoon arrived in Peebles and was instantly placed under security restrictions. He was not allowed to see any patient records, and was restricted to watching the gate and cleaning the latrines. The hospital was used by Rosyth naval base and the records could reveal information about the location of ships and units. Roland went AWOL, was arrested, and sentenced to twenty-seven days in the military wing of Barlinnie Prison. Anderson was given the job of guarding the prisoner en route to Glasgow.

During the journey Roland pointed out his duelling scars, where he had been 'blooded' during an initiation ceremony admitting him to a right-wing society when he was at university in Germany. He told Anderson that he had been in the Hitler Youth, and had only got out of Germany thanks to the efforts of 'Winnie and Anthony'. Not that he thought getting out of Germany was necessarily a good thing, for he believed Nazism would triumph. 'If you give the British working man enough money for his cinema tickets, his football pools, a few pints and his cigarettes,' Roland said, 'that's all he's interested in. You've got him.'

Anderson found him aloof, arrogant, yet well educated. But in spite of keeping himself apart from the despised working-class sailors and soldiers at Peebles, Roland did have something of a social life off duty. He was a frequent dinner guest at the home of Captain Archibald Maule Ramsay, who was currently interned as a Nazi sympathiser and security risk. Roland appears to have been the guest of someone Anderson described as, 'a rather beautiful, well-dressed woman, who was a relative of Ramsay's'.

The Peebles MP began his political life as a rather parochial, run-of-the-mill member of the House, whose main interests seem to have been centred on his constituency. He was well liked by his fellows in the tea rooms and bars, and well regarded by his constituents. He appeared both affable and charming, though not, perhaps, the sharpest intellect in Westminster. Yet he turned, within a few years, into a rabid anti-Semite and a pro-Nazi, willing to deal with the enemy in time of war.

The trigger for this alarming change was the Spanish Civil War. Until the outbreak of the conflict he had contented himself with interventions concerning the state of the roads in Midlothian, or the drains in Peebles. When the war came his interventions turned to Spain, international Communist conspiracies, media bias in favour of the Republic and the Jews. What lay behind his strong pro-Franco line was religion, and what he first saw as a Bolshevik plot to undermine Christianity soon became that most Hitlerian of paranoias, a Communist–Jewish plot against the Aryan race.

Franco himself had billed his rebellion as a 'crusade' against atheism. This view was, in fact, dividing the strong and well-organised Catholic vote in the west of Scotland. Agitation on behalf of Nationalist Spain was strongly backed by some wealthy Scots Catholic families, and enjoyed some success. The prominent publicist Professor Charles Sarolea, a Belgian subject who lived in Edinburgh, was active in pro-Franco and pro-Nazi organisations, as was the retired Edinburgh university principal, and expert on the chemistry of Renaissance paint, A.P. Laurie. Ramsay was not a Catholic, but saw, in Spain, a common cause.

The first of the many groups Ramsay set up was the United Christian Front, designed to 'confront the widespread attack upon the Christian verities which emanates from Moscow and which is revealing itself in this country in a literary and educational campaign of great intensity'. The group attracted such luminaries as the Earl of Home, the Earl of Dalhousie, Lord Ruthven and the Episcopal Bishop of Brechin. A proposal for a Freethinkers' Conference in London, which Ramsay dubbed the 'League of the Militant Godless', found him proposing a private member's bill with the curious title of the Aliens Restriction (Blasphemy) Bill, designed to 'prevent the participation by aliens in assemblies propagating blasphemous

or atheistic doctrines or in other activities calculated to inter-
fere with the established religious institutions of Great Britain'.
It never made the statute book, but did pass its first reading.

One has the impression of a man who had existed on a fairly
mundane and fairly reasonable plateau stepping off and falling
into an increasingly mad vortex of unreason. In early 1937 in
the House of Commons he raised allegations of anti-Franco
bias in the BBC. Within a year, however, he introduced
another private member's bill, the innocuous-sounding Companies Act (1929) Amendment, a fully-fledged attempt to
legislate against what, in his opening speech, he characterised
as 'sinister international forces who could cause war, financial
disaster and other political crises' seeking to control the media.
He referred to sinister forces, New York financiers and Big
Finance, all well-understood code words for the Jews, seeking
to manipulate and control news for their own ends.

He practised one of the strangest pieces of doublethink
common to the far right of the 1930s in holding that the
perceived Jewish threat came from the super-rich, whilst
believing that part and parcel of the same plot was Soviet
Communism. In a letter to the *Scotsman* in January 1939 he
gave his view on the composition of the Central Committee of
the Communist Party, citing one of his favourite works: 'The
Jewish complexion of the body is clearly set out in a booklet
published on March 26, 1938, entitled "Rulers of Russia". It
is written by the Rev. Denis Fahey, CSSP, and bears the
imprimatur of the Archbishop of Dublin. It states that of
the 59 members of the central Committee of the Communist
Party in 1935, 56 were Jews, and the remaining 3, namely
Stalin, Lobow and Ossinsky, were married to Jewesses.'

In Ramsay's eyes Hitler was the bulwark both against

Communism, and against the Jews. The *Arbroath Herald* reported a speech he gave to the town's Business Club in 1938, on the 'Jewish' nature of the Third International: 'His [Hitler's] antipathy to the Jews is caused by his complete belief in the knowledge that the real power behind the Third International is a group of revolutionary Jews who have joined all organisations throughout the world.'

Yet it would be wrong to think of Ramsay as simply a deranged paranoiac ploughing a lonely furrow. His Companies Act bill, like his Aliens and Blasphemy bill, failed to reach the statute book, but did make it through its first reading, and attracted support from mainstream Tories as well as from the far right usual suspects of the day. It is true that his Right Club attracted a superabundance of aristocrats as fellow travellers. Richard Griffiths, author of *Patriotism Perverted*, unearthed the membership list – Ramsay's so-called Red Book. It shows that, besides the father of Diana Mosley and Unity Mitford, Lord Redesdale, the fifth Duke of Wellington, Lord Sempill and the Earl of Galloway were also members. The Nordic League, an 'association of race-conscious Britons' to which Ramsay belonged, was infiltrated by Inspector Pavey, an ex-officer of the Special Branch, who reported on meetings of two hundred with 'a fair sprinkling of women, obviously of the upper classes'.

It would be wrong, too, to assume that support for the Nazis was confined to the upper middle classes and aristocracy, or was the sole province of Tory right wingers. Sir Oswald Mosley, leader and founder of the British Union of Fascists, had, after all, been a Labour minister in the Macdonald government. Although Mosley was electorally unsuccessful in Scotland, the leading elite of the BUF included the former

Labour figures, Dr Robert Forgan, John Scanlon and Charles Raven Thomson. A.P. Laurie was a Liberal and an associate of Lloyd George, whose meeting with Hitler in 1937 he had helped to arrange. One of the twelve MPs who were members of the Right Club was Sir Ernest Bennett, the National Labour MP for Cardiff Central, whose primary concern was the Arab cause in Palestine, and a wish to cement relations with Nazi Germany as a bulwark against Communism. He relegated persecution of the Jews to a position of relative unimportance in his view of the greater scheme of things.

The Nazis themselves had a particular interest in Scotland, viewing the Scots as Celts, ethnically distinct from the English, who could be detached from Britain. German intellectuals had a long-standing interest in Scottish culture, dating back to the eighteenth century when Herder lauded the epic nature of the Ossianic poems 'discovered' by James Macpherson. Haydn and Beethoven both arranged Scottish folk songs, and the latter used an Irish tune as the starting point for the main theme of the finale of his seventh symphony. Goethe had written to Thomas Carlyle in the 1820s about the distinctive nature of the Scots. Carlyle, whose racism reflected strong anti-Irish feeling in west central Scotland, was popular with the Nazis and their sympathisers on this side of the North Sea. William Joyce ('Lord Haw-haw'), the thuggish intellectual who was to go on to gain notoriety and execution for treason for his wartime broadcasts from Berlin, was a member of the Carlyle Club, a far-right discussion group.

The Scottish literary renaissance of the 1920s and '30s intrigued Nazi intellectuals. Its authoritarian leader, Hugh MacDiarmid, was at one time a enthusiast for Mussolini, although he later transferred his power-worship to Stalin rather than to Hitler. The salience of themes to do with peasantry and the land chimed in with Nazi preoccupations with 'Blood and Soil' and Heimat. There were corporatist tendencies in the ideas of Compton Mackenzie and Ronald Macdonald Douglas, and a lunatic nationalist fringe so neatly satirised by Evelyn Waugh in *Officers and Gentlemen*: 'When the Germans land in Scotland the glens will be full of marching men come to greet them, and the professors themselves at the universities will seize the towns. Mark my words, don't be caught on Scottish soil that day.'

There was a division of the Abwehr, the Nazi military intelligence service, responsible for subversion among minorities under a Major Voss. This was to be the template, as we shall see, for thinking within MI6 and US intelligence at the beginning of the Cold War. According to Professor Chris Harvie of Tübingen University, one early contact was by an academic, Hans Galinsky, who met several leaders of the Scottish renaissance in the early 1930s. Galinsky also believed there was serious discussion within the Nazi Party as to whether the Celts could be considered as part of the Volk, but it was decided that they were altogether too dangerous and unstable to be admitted to that unholy tribe. In 1936 extreme right-wing nationalists, such as Ronald Macdonald Douglas, were invited to the Nuremberg Rally.

Hitler's interpreter at that rally was Erich Hetzler, an SS officer who was, at the time, Ribbentrop's propaganda specialist at the London Embassy. Hetzler, described by Goebbels as a 'clever, shrewd propagandist, completely in agreement with our reasoning', went on to run the Nazis' secret radio stations. During the war these stations transmitted 'black' propaganda, seeking to appear as if they were broadcasting from within the target country. One of the stations was to be 'Radio Caledonia', which broadcast a Scottish separatist message; another, the New British Broadcasting Station, pitched its message at Ramsay's right-wing constituency.

Contacts were also made in 1936 and 1937 by the Gesellschaft für Keltische Studien, one of those curious academic organisations established by the Nazis for political and cultural purposes. It was led by Professor Ludwig Mulhausen, a party member and an expert on Irish Gaelic, who had learned the language in County Kerry in the early 1930s. He was to head the Irish service of the Reichsrundfunk during the war and broadcast a commentary in Irish every Sunday evening for the duration, and was assisted by the prominent Irish novelist Francis Stuart, who taught at Berlin University as a neutral throughout the conflict.

The Gesellschaft carried out academic work, particularly Mulhausen's own projects on philology and his collection of folk tales from the west of Ireland, though much of this was tinged with a vaguely romantic racist culturalism. It is little wonder that many members spent a considerable time mulling over the Scottish renaissance. Indeed the renaissance came to Berlin, as the novelist Neil Gunn, a prominent SNP member, used to spend the summers throughout the 1930s staying in the Kempinski Hotel, living off royalties which he was not allowed to take out of the Reich. The Gesellschaft was deeply involved in political analyses of the Celtic nationalist movements in Ireland, Wales, Brittany and Scotland.

This was a sensitive time for the fledgling Scottish National Party, formed by the amalgamation of the National Party of Scotland with the more right-wing Scottish Party in 1934. It was embroiled in an acrimonious debate between fundamentalists who modelled themselves on Sinn Fein, and moderates willing to ally with Labour and Liberals. Led by John MacCormick, one of the founders of the NPS in 1928, they seemed to be winning when in 1937 the SNP voted against conscription. This must have seemed like good news to members of the Gesellschaft, who were at the time on one of their fact-finding missions to Scotland.

The Nazis, then, waged their 1930s propaganda campaign in Britain on a wide front, from attempting to influence the Celtic nationalist parties, through encouraging various peace movements, to contact with actual dyed-in-the-wool fellow travellers like Ramsay. The key year was 1938, the year of the Anschluss, Munich and of the Kristallnacht pogrom.

When the Duchess of Atholl moved from being a rebel who resigned the whip to being deselected by her local constituency it was no mere parochial issue involving Kinross and West Perthshire, or even Scottish politics. The Munich Agreement, which gave Hitler the Sudetenland and effectively sealed the fate of Czechoslovakia, provoked a crisis within the Conservative Party. The duchess was not alone amongst the anti-appeasement MPs in facing constituency problems. Robert Boothby in East Aberdeenshire, Richard Law in Hull, Duff Cooper in Westminster, Cranborne in South Dorset and Wolmar in Aldershot faced battles with their local Conservative Associations. Most remarkable of all was that over a period of six weeks following the Munich debate in the House, Winston Churchill himself faced the prospect of deselection.

The duchess was deselected over the bizarre accusation that she had sung 'The Red Flag' at a public meeting in Glasgow on Basque asylum seekers. The constituency meeting at which this was carried out was held whilst she was in London, with no chance of returning to Atholl to fight her corner. They took some time to find a candidate and the smears continued. A story was circulated that a charity she was involved in to help people disabled in the Spanish Civil War was actually a recruiting organisation for the International Brigades, and thereby contravened the Foreign Enlistment Act. A speech she made in the US, innocuous to the point of boredom, was reported to the Constituency Association as 'blackening the name of Great Britain'. On 31 May she wrote in fury to the local newspaper, the *Perth Constitutional*: 'Captain Luttman-Johnson is again interfering in the affairs of a constituency of which he is not an elector.' This was in reference to the accusation that she had introduced as speakers 'men who have served in the International Brigades and who were said to have been in serious conflict with the forces of the Crown'.

Luttman-Johnson, an acolyte of Captain Ramsay's, was a retired Indian Army officer with an estate near Perth. He had been secretary of the January Club, one of those innumerable far-right societies of the 1930s, the purpose of this particular one being to act as a respectable front for Mosley's British Union of Fascists. When that folded he formed a discussion group for upper class neo-Nazis known as the Windsor Club, before becoming a leading light in the Scottish branch of the pro-Franco Friends of National Spain and a member of the Right Club.

Luttman-Johnson was a Germanophile, an enthusiast for Nietzschian philosophy and ideas of the superman, afraid of the Asiatic hordes of Russian Communists stirring up the rabble and destroying civilisation, an old military man who was enthused by the crash of jackboots along Unter den

Linden, the Panzers revving their engines on Luneburg Heath, and the Stukas wailing out of clear blue skies. Letters from him, seized by MI5, reveal that he signed off those to his pro-Nazi friends with 'Heil Hitler'. The Duchess of Atholl decided that the proper course of action was to resign her seat and fight the resulting by-election as an Independent. Richard Griffiths tells us that on 1 July, just after she made the announcement, Ramsay phoned Luttman-Johnson to suggest that he should contest the seat. He himself preferred to continue to work in the shadows.

The Tories choose a local laird, McNair Sneddon, as their candidate. He was a somewhat colourless man, who would toe the Chamberlain line and was destined to leave no mark on the political landscape. The local Liberals adopted a Mrs 'Coll' Macdonald, but the party decided at a national level not to contest the seat, as did the Labour Party. It became a straight fight between the Duchess of Atholl, standing as an Independent, and the official Conservative candidate.

In her speeches and election manifesto she warned of the dangers of appeasement, of the need to draw a line in the sand in concert with France and Russia to halt Hitler's territorial ambitions, the need for rearmament, and, 'on the advice of a very distinguished general', to establish a Ministry of Supply to oversee procurement. It was a fundamentally Churchillian manifesto. He telephoned her most evenings and sent her a letter of support: 'The issues raised by your candidature go far beyond ordinary questions of parliamentary or party affairs . . . You stand for the effective rearmament of our country . . . the creation of a Ministry of Supply, which you have advocated, would be a welcome symbol of earnestness and energy which would not fail to make an impression upon foreign countries. Your victory as an Independent member adhering to the first principles of the Conservative and Unionist Party can only have an invigorating effect upon the whole impulse of Britain's policy and Britain's defence.'

She felt pretty confident of victory, boosted by large numbers of anti-appeasment speakers of all political hues who made the journey north to back her. As she later admitted, however, she underestimated the myth of Chamberlain as the saviour of peace, and that to query the Munich agreement was to be branded a warmonger. The message did the rounds – that a vote for the duchess was a vote for war. On 21 December the electorate delivered their verdict: she was defeated by a margin of 11,808 votes to 10,495, and the colourless Chamberlain yes-man won by 1,313 votes. Had the election taken place just a few months later, after Hitler had swallowed the rest of Czechoslovakia, then the outcome might have been very different.

She was devastated. She returned to Atholl Palace. On that still, cold night of defeat, as the snow fell on the woods and mountains of the estate, for the first time in years she sat before the piano and played Beethoven's *Appassionata* sonata, 'which I had long, alas, neglected'. She then turned to his *Waldstein* sonata. A few miles away Luttman-Johnson raised a glass to celebrate her defeat. The pro-Nazi Germanophile would have approved of her choice of music.

It is impossible to say how much the Ramsay faction influenced other deselection battles, none of which resulted in by-elections. Churchill's does, however, have one interesting feature in this regard. The leader of the faction attempting to oust him from his Epping constituency was Colin Thornton-Kemsley, then an Essex estate agent. Churchill forced a ballot within his local Executive and secured a vote of 100 to 40 in his favour, finally seeing off any deselection threat. Thornton-Kemsley did not belong to any pro-Nazi organisation, but he had married into the minor Scottish aristocracy and moved in the rarefied atmosphere inhabited by Ramsay fellow-travellers. In 1939 he became MP for Kincardine and West Aberdeenshire, of the right-wing nonentity variety, remembered by Lord Jenkins as, 'a small, dark, moustachioed Conservative backbencher trying without much success to make an impact upon the House of Commons'.

The war, when it came, saw a flurry of increasingly secret meetings amongst the various pro-Nazi groups – at least they thought they were secret. The Right Club was infiltrated by no fewer than four MI5 agents, Marjorie Amor (real name Mrs Marjorie Mackie), Helene de Munk, Joan Miller and Philip Brocklehurst. There was also a more freelance penetration by Captain J. Hughes, alias Captain P.G. Taylor of the British Union, who had acted as a Special Branch informer on BU activities. Ramsay used Hughes as his representative at a number of these meetings. Given that these 'secret' meetings were often of extremely small groups, one wonders how often the Security Services outnumbered the genuine activists.

Special Branch reports of the time paint a sometimes alarming picture: 'From two independent sources we learn that the activity of the Right Club is centred principally upon the contacting of sympathisers, especially among officers in the armed services, and the spreading by personal talks of the Club's ideals. There is talk of a military coup d'état, but there seems to be a lack of agreement amongst members on the question of leadership. Sir Oswald Mosley they regard with suspicion.'

The idea of a coup seems to be fanciful in the extreme, but the dissemination of subversive ideas was quite another matter. They mainly concentrated on anti-Semitic themes. Ramsay produced a dreadful ditty entitled 'Land of Dope and Jewry'. His pamphlet on International Jewry and the War stated that: 'the stark truth is that this war was plotted and engineered by Jews for world power and vengeance'.

This propaganda did not fall on exactly deaf ears. There was a growing belief that Jewish refugees from the Third Reich constituted a kind of fifth column, and were harming the war effort. In October 1939 a *Daily Mail* columnist wrote that he believed many enemy agents had come to the UK as refugees and that 'many of these alien immigrants are Jews. They should be careful not to arouse the same resentment here as they have stirred up in so many countries.' The resignation, in January 1940, of the Secretary of State for War, Leslie Hore-Belisha, had little to do with race and more to do with his dreadful relations with the General Staff. Nevertheless, the proposal to appoint him as Minister of Information was blocked by the senior Civil Service, who nicknamed him Horeb, largely because he was a Jew. His time at the War Ministry also produced this populist marching song:

> Onward Christian Soldiers,
> You have nought to fear,
> Israel Hore Belisha
> Will lead you from the rear.
> Clothed by Monty Burton,
> Fed on Lyons pies,
> Die for Jewish freedom,
> As a Briton always dies.

In February 1940 Hetzler's New British Broadcasting Station, the NBBS, went onto the airwaves, with its pretence of coming from somewhere in England. Each broadcast began with the playing of 'The Bonnie Banks o' Loch Lomond' and ended with 'God save the King'. A BBC report noted: 'It has produced many stunts, including the purported revelation of General Ironside's report on the difficulties of repulsing invasion, a report on the proceedings of a secret meeting of the British Government at which the station's activities were supposed to have been discussed, revelations of German invasion plans, first aid hints (in the course of which the opportunity was taken to describe in a very gruesome manner the type of casualties which would result from German air raids) and code messages to alleged supporters in this country.'

Hetzler circulated a report to his staff from an agent, identified only as A.T., who was probably an Irish source. A.T. was in London at this period and listened to the NBBS. He reported that listening times and wavelengths were being advertised by gummed stickers 'all along Whitehall', and that the ruse that the station was coming from within the UK was working to the extent that 'some' of his contacts believed one of the broadcasters was Ramsay.

In fact, it is clear from BBC surveys that almost all of the small number of listeners to NBBS were in no doubt that the broadcasts came from Berlin. The sticker campaign, however, was real enough. Ramsay's self-styled aide-de-camp in 1940 was Anna Wolkoff, the daughter of a White Russian family who ran a tea-room in Kensington. Wolkoff produced a guide to planting the leaflets, advising her operatives to work in pairs, to walk on the dark side of the street and to watch out for policemen in unlit doorways.

She it was who first made contact with Tyler Kent, a cipher clerk at the American Embassy in London, thus becoming the nemesis of the Right Club. Kent had been under surveillance since he had been spotted passing a package to a known Gestapo agent, Ludwig Matthias, at the Cumberland Hotel. Matthias, a naturalised Swede, had been staked out almost since the moment he stepped on British shores.

Kent was an isolationist who believed the US should stay out of European wars. Although anti-Semitic, it is unclear whether the motivation for his activities was Communist or Nazi. He had been at the embassy in Moscow, and after the war the FBI reclassified him as a Soviet spy. In 1940, however, this did not greatly matter as this was the period of the Nazi–Soviet non-aggression pact and the carve-up of Poland.

He was intercepting correspondence between Ambassador Joe Kennedy and the British Foreign Secretary Lord Halifax, between Kennedy and President Roosevelt and, most importantly, communications between Churchill and Roosevelt. As America was neutral at this stage, these latter were so secret, involving as they did early discussions about the possibility of the US giving Britain destroyers, that not even the Foreign Office knew about them. Wolkoff and Ramsay became frequent visitors to Kent's flat, and it is probable that the young American and the White Russian had a sexual relationship. He was a well-known womaniser; Malcom Muggeridge described him as 'one of these intensely gentlemanly Americans who wear well-cut tailor-made suits, with waistcoat and watch chain'.

Ramsay was astonished by the documents, and later claimed he intended to raise the Churchill/Roosevelt correspondence in parliament, but had taken a short holiday before he could bring the matter to the floor of the House. At this point it depends on which of this nest of spies and pro-Nazis you want to believe. What happened was that Wolkoff took two of the documents, had them copied, and passed them to a contact of hers at the Italian Embassy, the Duco del Monte, who was the Naval Attaché. Italy at the time was still neutral, but, of course, happily passed anything of use to the Nazis on to Berlin. Is Ramsay's claim that he took a short holiday and knew nothing of what his otherwise faithful aide-de-camp was up to credible? On the balance of probabilities, it seems unlikely.

Wolkoff was trapped by an MI5 operation. One of the problems in running a propaganda operation in wartime, particularly a radio station pretending to come from within your enemy's country, is getting good, believable information about what is happening on the ground, and getting feedback to develop specific hard-hitting lines. Wolkoff raised this issue with one of the Right Club members, Joan Miller, an MI5 plant. She told Miller she had a coded letter for William Joyce, already notorious as 'Lord Haw-haw', but she couldn't get it out because her Italian contact was ill. The MI5 sting, after they had ascertained the letter did, in fact, only refer to propaganda feedback, was to let her pass the document to an agent the British Secret Service had in the Romanian Embassy. At the end of the letter was the codeword 'Carlyle', which Joyce was to use on a Thursday or Sunday broadcast to acknowledge receipt. When Joyce broadcast the acknowledgement, MI5 decided to act, and the Special Branch arrested Wolkoff and Kent. His diplomatic immunity was waived by the US, and, after separate trials, he was sentenced to seven years in prison and Wolkoff to ten.

Morningside Mata Haris

On the surface the Kent/Wolkoff affair was the catalyst which decided the Cabinet on strengthening the Defence of the Realm Act, allowing them to imprison the entire subversive far right. The decision was made two days after Kent's arrest, but in fact the whole war situation changed in May 1940. Since September 1939 there had been the 'Phoney War', when the French and British armies faced the Wehrmacht on the Western Front and nothing much happened.

On 10 May 1940 all that changed when the Germans launched 136 divisions and 2,500 aircraft in an operation that brought the world a new way of waging war, the Blitzkrieg. On 21 May, Wehrmacht troops reached the Channel coast at Le Crotoy. On the 24th Rommel wrote to his wife: 'My estimate is the war will be won in a fortnight.' Britain evacuated the remains of its army at Dunkirk. Within six weeks of the attack being launched France had fallen and 100,000 young men were dead. On 2 July Hitler ordered his forces to prepare to invade Britain, 'provided air superiority can be obtained and certain other necessary conditions fulfilled'.

In domestic politics the May Blitzkrieg swept away the Chamberlain government and brought in the wartime coalition under Churchill. What had been a war to stop Nazi aggression had become, in a few short weeks, a struggle for survival. The fall of France contained not only military lessons, but lessons on the importance of civilian morale. During the Phoney War, Goebbels had introduced a plethora of secret stations broadcasting Communist or petit-bourgeois messages in French. It aimed a station at Brittany, 'La Voix de Bretagne', projecting separatist demands, declaring the hour of liberation from the yoke of Paris was at hand. These stations, aided by

French Fascists in the cafés and on the streets, spread scare stories, and helped create a mood of panic and economic chaos. Rumours of devaluation sparked a run on the banks. There were suggestions that German–Jewish refugees were a fifth column of spies, bent on destruction and that (non-existent) French groups would stage a 'fight to the death' in Paris. All this helped create 'la Grande Peur' – the Great Fear – when around a quarter of Parisians abandoned the city. Potential subversion mattered to a nation facing invasion.

Within five days of coming to power, on 15 May, Churchill was apprised of MI5 thinking on the subversive right in a report on the 'Fifth Column Menace'. He was told it was believed by the Security Services that Wolkoff had given Berlin prior warning of that disastrous British adventure, the Narvik raid, and that Mosley and Ramsay were attempting to unify Nazis, Fascists and peace campaigners. The Home Secretary, Sir John Anderson, told Churchill that the Right Club was 'carrying on pro-German activities and secret subversive work, with the object of disorganising the Home Front'.

The defence regulations were strengthened at a secret meeting of the Privy Council and arrests began on 23 May. Ramsay spent most of the war in prison. Luttman-Johnson was arrested, but was released before the end of the conflict. He was unrepentant and sent grouse from his Perthshire estate to Ramsay in Brixton Prison. Ramsey himself became, if anything, more obsessive as time wore on. He continued to write anti-Semitic pamphlets until he died in 1955.

It is not recorded whether Kitty Atholl raised a glass when she heard her one-time tormentor, Luttman-Johnson, had been imprisoned. She was probably too occupied running a home for evacuee children at Blair Castle and organising Perthshire's civil defence. As the war progressed she was also falling into the orbit of those in and around MI6 planning a map of the post-war world.

Chapter Four

Hot to Cold

Old intelligence hands, though not those who belonged to MI6, often said the greatest mistake inflicted upon the British Secret Services was the abolition at the end of the Second World War of the SOE, the Special Operations Executive. The Executive was set up by Churchill and charged to 'go and set Europe ablaze'. As much as anything, he set it up because he did not wholly trust the coterie of former public schoolboys who largely ran MI6. MI6, for its part, despised SOE from the start as a bunch of amateurs, and rejoiced at its destruction at the end of hostilities.

MI6 were happy enough, however, to bask in the reflected glory of another group they despised as amateurs. For more than thirty years the breaking of the German Enigma codes was an official secret, and a secret kept by the vast army of academics, mathematicians, crossword setters and number crunchers who worked at Bletchley Park. The Ultra material, as it was called, was handled by MI6, and specifically by its head, Sir Stewart Menzies, to make it seem as if our spies had done an amazing job during the Second World War, when the work had actually been done by a bunch of often eccentric eggheads in a requisitioned English country house. Whether this piece of spin had anything to do with the Enigma story being kept a secret for such an inordinate length of time is a very moot point.

One operation conducted by MI6 had its origin, strange as it may sound, in a plan to virtually re-create the Hapsburg Empire. In 1938, after the Anschluss, when Austria was incorporated into the Reich, MI6 recruited agents within monarchist cells which had made contact with Britain and France. This was no off-the-wall piece of espionage. The idea of a Danubian Federation, stretching from the Aegean to the Baltic, under the Hapsburgs, had the support of no less a person than Winston Churchill, who for a time had been a member of the Pan-European Union. This right-wing organisation had been founded in 1923 by the Hapsburg Count Coudenhove-Kalergi, who believed such a confederation would act as a curb on Russian expansion.

This conception was the germ of what was to be the world view of MI6 for some twenty years, developed, with journalist and sometime spy F.A. Voigt in his Middle Zone Association, and, as the war progressed, quietly dropping the anachronistic Hapsburg involvement. In a 1942 editorial in his *Nineteenth Century and After*, which one might almost call the MI6 house journal, Voigt outlined the evolving thoughts on the shape of post-war Europe. Poland was to be the principal power in what he described as the Northern Group of the Middle Zone, a role to be fulfilled by Czechoslovakia in the Central Group, consisting of herself, Austria and Hungary. The Czechs, however, would have to 'extirpate Pan-Germanism in Austria'. The Southern Group was to be the Balkans, under the leadership of Yugoslavia. The idea was not at all a bad one; the trouble was that it was used as a propaganda hook to bring on board some extremely dubious organisations and individuals.

Intermarium – a word meaning between the seas – was an organisation founded by Tsarists in the 1930s; before the war it had received funds from MI6 and the backing of the Vatican. It brought together émigré leaders from eastern Europe, and had the decided whiff of fascism and militant Catholic anti-Semitism about it. According to Michael Herman's paper, 'The Role of Military Intelligence after 1945', when the the Nazis invaded the Soviet Union, Intermarium 'became an instrument of German intelligence'. As the Reich collapsed and the Red Army rolled ever westward MI6 revived its contacts and its funding.

The Promethean League was, if anything, an even more morally dubious organisation. Created after the First World War, it originally represented all the ethnic minorities within the Soviet Union, but rapidly became dominated by Ukrainian and, to a lesser extent, Georgian nationalists. MI6 began to support and finance the League in 1925 in Paris, where the operation was run by Stewart Menzies, at the time a humble agent working in the French capital. The trouble with the Ukrainian nationalists was that they too often took to heart the dangerous old dictum, 'my enemy's enemy is my friend'.

From the late 1920s onwards the Promethean League also maintained contacts, and took cash, from German Intelligence. When the Nazis came to power these activities were stepped up. In the inter-war years the western Ukraine was in Polish hands, and the Abwehr saw an opportunity for espionage in both Poland and the USSR by playing the Ukrainian nationalist card. The League became increasingly authoritarian and anti-Semitic in character; following the invasion of the Soviet Union they threw in their lot with the Germans, in common with large numbers – probably a majority – of their fellow nationalists. In 1943 a Ukrainian division of the SS – the Galizien Division – was formed and developed a reputation for ruthlessness in actions against partisans and the mass murder of Jews as ferocious as any in Himmler's black tribe. As Nazi Germany collapsed, MI6 reactivated contact with League members; as for the fate of the Galizien Division, most of the survivors, as we shall see, settled in the UK.

The besetting problem of Ukrainian nationalism was factionalism. The inter-war incorporation of western Ukraine – Galicia – into Poland created an even more extreme organisation than the Promethean League: the OUN (Organisation of Ukrainian Nationalists). Warsaw had a deal of sympathy with the League, particularly if it restricted its campaign to the liberation of that part of the Ukraine within the Soviet Union. The OUN, however, was both anti-Russian and anti-Polish. It was a terrorist organisation, whose model was the IRA, and it was outlawed by the League of Nations. The organisation was responsible for a number of attacks on Polish politicians and officials, culminating in the murder of the Interior Minister General Peiracki in 1934. Throughout this period MI6 was using the OUN for espionage purposes within the USSR through its station in Finland. The OUN was, however, also hand in glove with Nazi Intelligence. It is unclear, but quite possible that MI6 and the Abwehr may have co-operated in Ukrainian operations pre-1939.

The most significant post-war leader to emerge from the OUN was Stefan Bandera, according to Kim Philby a 'darling of the British'. Prior to the Nazi invasion of the Soviet Union Bandera's OUN group was heavily funded by the Abwehr and trained by the Gestapo. In April 1941 it was organised into two units codenamed 'Nachtigall' and 'Roland'. When Operation Barbarossa was launched, Roland advanced with the Wehrmacht to Bessarabia, whilst Nachtigall remained closer to home and joined the Nazi advance on Lviv. When the city fell the unit enthusiastically joined in the ensuing pogrom. The speciality of the Nachtigall unit was to heap men, women and children – around eighty at a time – into trenches and grenade them. The Ukrainian Military Police were attached to Einsatz-gruppen C, one of the Nazi killing squads that roamed the Eastern Front shooting in the back of the neck Jews, gypsies, Communists and others deemed sub-human. The Ukrainians specialised in the murder of children. Bandera's right-hand man and staunchest supporter was at Lviv one Yaroslav Stetzko – he was to become a frequent visitor to the Scottish League for European Freedom in Edinburgh and a 'dear friend' of its chairman, John Finlay Stewart.

On 30 June 1941 Stetzko opened a 'National Assembly' in Lviv, which proclaimed an independent Ukraine allied to the Reich. Hitler, however, reneged on the agreement between the OUN and the Abwehr that in return for their military support the Ukrainians would be allowed a degree of autonomy. Two thousand OUN supporters were arrested and Bandera and Stetzko were interned at Sachsenhausen concentration camp, but with privileged status.

Things changed again, however, as the war progressed. Yet another faction emerged, the UPA, the Ukrainian Insurgent Army. In 1943, as the tide of war turned decisively against the Reich, large numbers of other ethnic minorities from within the Soviet Union went over to this organisation 'to form a national formation of enslaved peoples'. Nazi Intelligence saw here an opportunity to create a partisan movement around the USSR, and through the OUN funded an 'Anti-Bolshevik

Front'. This was the forerunner of the Anti-Bolshevik Bloc of Nations, the ABN, another organisation resurrected by MI6 in 1945.

The final link in this chain was the innocuous-sounding Central European Federal Study Clubs, which were basically the sponsoring agency for Intermarium. The president of the London club was Count August Zaleski, Foreign Minister and later President of the Polish government in exile. What this network needed was a front organisation, distanced from the émigré groups, where Intelligence work could be carried out in the background, assets identified, and propaganda disseminated. This was to be the Scottish League for European Freedom.

As the final year of the war came, the hope that the peace settlement would result in an East European Confederation was evaporating by the day. The reality on the ground was the Red Army, and the birth of the Soviet Empire was being mapped out at the series of conferences held by the soon to be victorious powers. Yet Churchill still clung to the idea of the Danubian Federation. In 1944 he had set up a Central European Committee to examine the nuts and bolts of the concept, and as late as early 1945 was still enthused by the idea.

Sir Owen O'Malley, British Ambassador to the Polish government in exile, was more realistic. The idea that the Soviet Union was going to allow the formation of any kind of autonomous federation in the areas it held he dismissed as 'Alice in Wonderland'. As early as 1943 he warned against what was now, in 1945, coming to pass: the acceptance by the West of Soviet predominance in certain areas. 'At what cost in human values,' he wrote, 'would not the sovietisation of central and south-eastern Europe be achieved?' The 'surrender to the cruel and heathenish tyranny of the Soviets of a large part of the heritage of Roman and Byzantine civilisation', was, he believed, a morally unsustainable position.

Churchill had wanted to hold the Yalta Conference, which fashioned the shape of the new Europe, in the autumn of 1944, before Soviet troops entered the countries of eastern Europe. He failed, and it was held in February 1945. Promises extracted from Stalin to hold free elections, particularly in the case of Poland, were to prove hollow. The Soviets had already established a puppet government to put in place when Poland finally fell, and the Polish government in exile in London was being consigned to a footnote in history. The Eastern Bloc was being born, not an East European Federal Union.

Poland haunted Churchill. He set out his fears in a telegram to the US President Harry S. Truman in early May: 'I feel deep anxiety because of the Soviets misinterpretation of the Yalta decisions, their attitude towards Poland, their overwhelming influence in the Balkans, excepting Greece . . . the combination of Russian power and the territories under their control or occupied, coupled with the Communist technique in so many other countries, and above all their power to maintain very large armies in the field for a long time . . . An iron curtain is drawn down upon their line. We do not know what is going on behind.'

The Third World War could have started on 1 July 1945. Operation Unthinkable was an extraordinary plan which Churchill ordered the Joint Planning Staff to draw up for an attack on the Soviet Union on that date. The purpose was 'to impose upon Russia the will of the United States and British Empire. Even though the will of these countries may be defined as no more than a square deal for Poland, that does not necessarily limit the military commitment.'

It was drawn up under the direct control of General 'Pug' Ismay, Secretary to the Chiefs of Staff, circulation was strictly limited, and it was delivered to the prime minister on 22 May, just five days after the German surrender. It would probably have fallen at its very first hurdle, the opening assumption that the attack would be 'undertaken with the full support of public opinion'. This already difficult proposition, given four years of sustained gallant Russian ally propaganda, would not have been aided by the proposal to rearm 100,000 former Wehrmacht soldiers as part of the project. Indeed steps had already been taken to make this feasible, as Field Marshal Montgomery had been ordered by Churchill to store captured German weapons so they could be easily issued to German soldiers should the need arise. The report viewed such troops as being of poor value. The apparent advantage of knowing the territory, would, in fact, have been no advantage at all, as they would be fighting over old ground where they had sustained heavy defeats and losses in terrible conditions and, as such, would present a major risk to morale.

The planners estimated – and Intelligence on the Red Army was of a high order at this stage – that the Soviet strength would be 170 divisions, of which 30 would be armoured, which would mean British and US forces would be 'facing odds of the order of two to one in armour and four to one in infantry'. The planners also respected the toughness of the average Red Army soldier and 'bold tactics based largely on disregard for losses in attaining a set objective'. Old views that the Soviets had technologically poor equipment were also swept away: 'it moves on a lighter scale of maintenance than any Western Army . . . equipment has improved throughout the war and is now good'.

Indeed, technology has been underestimated as a factor in the Soviet victory on the Eastern Front. When the Wehrmacht roared into the USSR they seemed to do so with a glittering array of state-of-the-art armoured technology. That became part of their problem. Two thousand different types of vehicle thundered across the steppes in 1941, a spare part and main-tenance nightmare, over hard terrain and long distances. The Soviet T-34 was built by using the best of proven tank engineering, which could be serviced with supporting mechanics in situ. The German Tigers and Panthers were minor masterpieces of technological innovation, which had to be transported back to Germany for anything but the most routine maintenance.

The one question mark raised by the Unthinkable plan as to the Red Army related to discipline and morale. There was a shortage of staff officers and mid-level commanders. Heavy casualties and the horrors of the campaign had led to a certain war weariness, and a breakdown of order. Looting, rape and drunkenness were now a commonplace in eastern Europe, in some places reducing the Red Army to a rabble.

One clear advantage to the Allies identified by the Unthink-able planners lay with the strategic bombing force, but even here the nature of the Eastern Front would have somewhat blunted its power. Soviet industry was dispersed and 'would not make a profitable air target'. However, the consequent long lines of communications appeared to offer 'far more favourable targets, especially at the important crossings of the river barriers'.

The prognosis was gloomy. Surprise would be a major

factor, but the best the planners could hope for was to get as 'far as Hitler did in 1941', the more likely outcome being a drive to the east for a line around Danzig/Breslau. They believed that unless the Soviets agreed to a favourable Polish settlement west of that line, 'we shall be committed to a total war'.

The Chiefs of Staff – Brooke, Cunningham and Tedder – were clearly appalled at the prospect of war with the Soviet Union in July 1945 and urged caution. Ismay wrote to Churchill laconically: 'by retaining the codeword Unthinkable, the Staffs will realise that this remains a precautionary study of what, I hope, is still a purely hypothetical contingency'. Churchill, of course, knew the great secret: that the Allies were preparing to test the first atomic bomb. The timing of Unthinkable is odd in the extreme. It is clear that Hitler's Barbarossa was delayed, and that delay was a factor in its ultimate failure, as 'General Winter' came to Stalin's aid before the very gates of Moscow. Yet that was launched on 22 June, and here was Churchill proposing an attack on 1 July.

It is unlikely we shall ever know just what was in Churchill's mind. Ismay circulated a note saying that the Chiefs of Staff 'have set out the bare facts', and, 'the less was put on paper, the better'. Brooke recorded Churchill's mood at the time: the prime minister 'now saw himself as the sole possessor of the bombs and capable of dumping them where he wished, thus all-powerful and dictating to Stalin'. Chemical and biological weapons may also have been on his mind, as they had been during the planning for the invasion of Europe. The first atomic bomb was tested just fifteen days after Unthinkable would have been launched, on 16 July, 1945.

Playing the nuclear card before the Soviet Union could

develop its own atomic bomb was to surface in Churchill's thoughts some time later. On 23 January 1948, when he was leader of the Opposition, he made a speech in the House of Commons calling on the Western democracies 'to bring matters to a head with the Soviet Union'. In Foreign Office papers released in 2003 it is clear his remarks caused concern with the Russia Committee, which had been set up to oversee the running of the Cold War. They sounded him out to seek clarification on what, exactly, he meant. 'Mr Churchill is in favour of a showdown . . . He emphasised the immense importance of the atomic bomb, and argued that the USA should use their monopoly of it to arrest the forward movement of the Soviet Union, as a policeman stops oncoming traffic' – a truly strange metaphor for nuclear weapons.

It would, in fact, have been the United States who would have killed Operation Unthinkable stone dead had it ever gone beyond the confines of a Whitehall discussion document. In the 1950s Churchill was to lament that 'Nothing would convince the Americans of the Russian danger.' Yet he had a curious view of Stalin. In October 1944 he had flown to Moscow, without informing the Americans, and without consulting his Cabinet, and had struck a percentages deal with Stalin. As he put it later in his war memoirs, he sat down with Stalin, and, when he felt the moment was right, said to the dictator, 'Let us settle our affairs in the Balkans. We have interests, missions and agents there. Don't let us get at cross purposes in small ways. So far as Britain and Russia are concerned, how would it do for you to have ninety per cent predominance in Romania, for us to have ninety per cent of the say in Greece, and go fifty-fifty about Yugoslavia?'

Stalin could be charming, a feature that makes him all the

more chilling a figure, and he charmed Churchill. According to Martin Gilbert's biography of Churchill, during the 1944 mission the two leaders drank long into the night. They cracked jokes, some of them extremely indiscreet. 'The trouble with the Poles,' Churchill said, 'was that they had unwise political leaders. Where there were two Poles there was one quarrel.'

'Where there was one Pole,' quipped the Soviet dictator, 'he would begin to quarrel with himself through sheer boredom.'

Churchill often remarked that Stalin had to watch out for the hard men of the Politburo, not, it seems, realising that it was Stalin himself who was the hardest man of all. The sense that the dictator was a man you could do business with, whilst the likes of Molotov were immovable objects of stone, did not arise because Uncle Joe was the more human individual – quite the reverse. It was because nobody dared second-guess Stalin lest, at best, they take the long walk to Siberia, or at worst, endure a night of torture followed by a bullet in the back of the neck at dawn.

In spite of their horror at the prospect of Operation Unthinkable the military were generally hawkish about the Soviet Union, deciding as early as 1943 that the next enemy would be the USSR. There is a racist tinge to many of their thoughts about the Russians which would not have been out of place in Berlin. The Chief of the General Staff, Field Marshal Sir Alan Brooke, called them 'this semi-Asiatic race with innate bargaining instincts'. The Foreign Office were generally the doves, and in 1943 did not believe that the Soviets would take over eastern Europe. Given the reality of 1945, this merely enhanced the view that the Foreign Office had been hopeless in their assessment of the threats of the 1930s, and were performing no better in the new landscape. Diplomats were divided, but the rule of thumb was that the closer the posting to dealing with the Soviet Union, the more likely you were to find a hawk.

As for MI6, they followed the military line from 1943 onwards: that the future enemy was likely to be the USSR. This was partly because Brooke and the other Chiefs of Staff imposed three service assistant directors on the organisation, partly because of the influx of personnel recruited from the military during the war and partly because it marked a return to business as usual. To British Intelligence in general the Soviet Union was the old enemy of Bolshevism and the Comintern.

Beneath the reflected glory of Ultra, MI6 was a shambles, a Byzantine court of seething rivalries and bitter office politics. Its head, Sir Stewart Menzies, was widely regarded as being somewhat intellectually challenged. He conducted much of his business over lunch at Whites, and his idea of recruiting staff was too often to tap the shoulder of a chum in the bar of a Pall Mall club. A former diplomat, Patrick Reilly, was appointed as a personal assistant and minder to Menzies in 1946, charged with instigating much-needed reforms. Richard Aldrich's book *The Hidden Hand* draws on material from Reilly, who discovered that MI6 dossiers contained 'prejudices, misrepresentations and downright falsehoods'.

In 1943 MI6 set up Section IX to take over Soviet operations. To run it they imported an MI5 agent called Currie, who was reaching retirement age and was hampered by deafness and a lack of knowledge of procedures. It was always understood that this was a temporary appointment and when the time came they made what must rank as one of the biggest Intelligence blunders in the history of an activity littered with blunders: they appointed Kim Philby. Britain entered the Cold War and MI6 had a Kremlin mole at the head of its Soviet section.

It became obvious at the Potsdam Conference in July 1945 that the wartime alliance with the USSR would not survive the peace. The personnel on the Western side changed. Roosevelt was dead, and his replacement was Harry Truman. Churchill and Clement Attlee, the Labour leader, returned to the UK halfway through the conference for the general election, and it was the victorious Attlee who came back with his new Foreign Secretary, Ernest Bevin. The Labour landslide produced huge and radical change on the domestic front, but in foreign policy the whole post-war approach was bipartisan. If anything Bevin was to prove the archetypal cold warrior; he had once told the Conservative politician, Douglas Dodds-Parker, 'You can leave Communism to me. I know all about it. I have been fighting it in the unions for thirty years.'

MI6 was putting in place the final touches to one of its weapons in this fight against Communism – the Intermarium-based network, designed to sow the seeds of ethnic and nationalist division within the emerging Soviet bloc and within the USSR itself. The remit of that original idea was already expanding to include plans to arm ethnic groups and to identify and equip émigrés who could be trained and sent back to the target areas. In the UK and around Europe the refugee camps were filling up with potential recruits, particularly if you did not look too closely at their past activities. It would seem that the Scottish League for European Freedom was not an existing organisation taken over by MI6, but was specifically set up to be the talent-spotting, UK-based propaganda centre for the network.

The Duchess of Atholl was drawn back into émigré affairs through her Polish contacts and through her friendship with Elma Dangerfield. Her beloved Bardie had died in 1942 and she had spent the war running her centre for evacuee children at Blair Castle and organising local civil defence on the Invasion Committee. She had also thrown herself into the 'Dig for Victory' campaign, digging up, 'with a heavy heart', much loved flowerbeds laid out for her by the duke and replanting them with vegetables.

From 1944 onwards a number of the émigrés from eastern Europe began to contact her. She recalled in her autobiography meeting Dr Gavrilovitch of the Yugoslav Peasants Party, and being told the British had withdrawn support for partisans fighting under General Mihailovich on behalf of King Peter and were instead backing Tito's Communists. The Polish prince and Princess Pusnya told her 'of their horror at the Great Powers' decision to hand over the eastern part of their country to the Russians'. An unnamed 'Latvian Minister', who 'happened to pay a visit to Birnham for the fishing', described to her the horrors of Soviet occupation and how many Latvians 'had fled to Sweden, some in open boats, to escape the Russians'.

She met an 'officer of the Polish Underground' who had recently been flown into the UK. He told her that members of the underground had received orders to reveal themselves to Red Army commanders as areas of the country were being 'liberated' by the Soviet advance, and to co-operate with the Russians in fighting the Nazis. Once the Germans had been driven out, the partisans were disarmed; the officers were packed off to Moscow and the rank and file given the choice of joining the Red Army or a small unit of pro-Communist Poles which had accompanied it. It was at this time that Elma Dangerfield was introduced to the duchess by Rowmund Pilsudski.

Pilsudski was a colourful character who was the cousin of Josef Pilsudski, one of the architects of Polish independence after the First World War. Josef had spent five years in a Siberian prison camp for his clandestine resistance work against the Tsarist Russian occupation prior to 1914. Rowmund had the fierce grey eyes and the courage of his famous relative and had fled Paris to join free Polish forces in the UK as a paratrooper. In 1944 he worked for the Polish government in exile's Information Department.

This has all the hallmarks of an intelligence set-up. The government in exile's Foreign Minister was August Zaleski, who was also president of that backbone of the Intermarium network, the Central European Federal Clubs. With F.A. Voigt, Dangerfield had set up the Middle Zone Association, which propagated the Central European federal line and had links of its own to MI6 through Voigt. The following month the first steps were taken at a meeting in Glasgow to set up the Scottish League.

Did the Duchess of Atholl know what its purpose was? Once again, it may be a case of the dog in the night not barking. In her autobiography she is vague in the extreme about the Scottish League, and indeed does not even mention it by name. In her campaigning work for east European refugees, she had, on a number of occasions, involved the Lord Provost of Glasgow, Sir Patrick Dolan. Dolan was

Labour's west of Scotland hardman and fixer, and he ran Scottish Socialism's heartland like a fiefdom.

What the duchess wrote of Scottish efforts to aid the Poles makes no mention of plans for a League, merely a committee with an unspecified remit: 'About the middle of September there was a big meeting in Glasgow on the international situation, at which Sir Patrick Dolan and I were among the speakers. The Lord Provost told us how he had first become interested in Poland from working beside Poles in the Scottish mines as a boy. He had learned from them of the tragic partition of their country in the eighteenth century, and so realised something of what it meant to them to be threatened once more with the loss of their precious freedom. He ended by telling us that he had set up a committee for its restoration.'

She goes on to claim that this inspired her to found the British League for European Freedom, but makes no mention of any Scottish sister organisation. Given that the SLEF's chairman was to be John Finlay Stewart, a long-standing friend of the duchess who affectionately called her Lady Kitty, this is somewhat disingenuous. An even larger dog that isn't barking is in Blair Atholl. In her private and political archive there are no files relating to the business of either League.

There is evidence that she was operating around the edges of espionage in the 1920s and '30s. As we shall see, the duchess became involved with one Intelligence network through a Russian émigré movement which supplied her with information on the Soviet Union. She was also acting in a low-key way on the domestic front collecting information on potentially subversive left-wing individuals and on Communist Party activity in the UK. She noted the activities of a front organisation for Soviet Intelligence, Arcos, which, according to her, 'is still the centre of Communist activities . . . large sums of money are transferred by Moscow to Arcos for the salaries of employees which never reach them and are transferred on to various Communist organisations.'

A particular area of her concern was Communist activity in the docks, naming George Hardy as 'being in charge of these operations, but apparently the progress, or lack of it, has displeased Moscow'. In June 1932 she was also contacted by a Mr E.A. Dickinson, who claimed to have been sent to Australia by the Communist Party at the behest of Moscow to assist in 'various forms of electoral corruption, such as the importation of workers into a constituency, who then became temporary electors for by-election purposes'. He was also one of the leaders of a dock strike in Sydney, and was imprisoned for nine months, after which he was sent to Glasgow to foment unrest in the shipyards. It would be unthinkable that a Conservative MP and former minister would not have passed on such information to the Security Services.

It would also be unthinkable that in 1945 the duchess would have rejected a discreet approach from MI6 to help them out by setting up a front in the shape of a charity. The ostensible reason for the meeting between the duchess, Pilsudski and Dangerfield was the Warsaw Rising. On 19 July 1944, encouraged by Soviet propaganda, and with Red Army tanks only twelve miles away, partisans and civilians, led by the Polish Underground Army, rose up and seized two thirds of the city from the Nazis. 'In many areas,' Julian Kulski wrote in his diary, 'the red and white flag of Poland is flying over our scarred and proud city for the first time in almost five years, and the hated Swastikas have been torn down and burnt.' To be fair to the tank commanders, who could hear the shooting coming from Warsaw, their advance was checked by German reinforcements and, outnumbered, they were forced to take up defensive positions – but not for over two months. There is no doubt that Stalin halted the advance to allow Warsaw, and the underground army loyal to the government in exile in London, to bleed to death.

Himmler gave the order to 'destroy tens of thousands'. One unit sent into the city was the Kaminski Brigade, made up of Cossacks, who were much feared for their ruthless anti-partisan and reprisal tactics. They were joined by the Dirle-wanger Brigade, a unit composed of hardened German crim-inals who had exchanged long prison sentences for duty on the Eastern Front. Stalin denied Britain and America the use of airfields just fifty miles from the city to facilitate drops of supplies to the Polish fighters. Without the bases the aircraft, flying from Italy, would be at the very limit of their operational range. Although too little, too late, the British and Americans went ahead anyway, using volunteer crews. Of the 360 aircraft dispatched, 41 were shot down, and some 200 aircrew killed. One American airman who bailed out was found by members of the Dirlewanger Brigade and beaten to death.

Pilsudski had been organising broadcasts to Warsaw through the BBC. According to the duchess, he first ap-proached Elma Dangerfield about the prospect of her making one aimed at the women of the city. By this time it was reckoned around 15,000 women and children had been killed by the Nazis. Dangerfield thought that she wasn't well known enough and Pilsudski suggested Kitty Atholl. This was the pretext for the three of them meeting at the offices of the Polish government in exile.

The duchess agreed to make the broadcast. 'I never heard,'

she wrote, 'if my message was received; as the days passed, the position of the Poles steadily became more hopeless, and, after nine weeks of terrible suffering, early in October, Warsaw surrendered.' Unfortunately, the broadcast has not been preserved in the BBC archives. She did go on to write one of the first accounts of the rising, *The Tragedy of Warsaw*, which is powerful and thoroughly researched, using British, Polish and German sources.

She had been 'deeply impressed' by the Glasgow meeting and felt 'efforts for Polish freedom should not be confined to Scotland'. She discussed the issue with Dangerfield who 'warmly approved', but whose knowledge of events in the Soviet Union led the duchess to believe: 'any organisation we formed should interest itself in all European countries where freedom was threatened . . . it was our duty as citizens of a free country to state the facts we knew.' The British League for European Freedom that grew out of these conversations was to have some rather strange characters associated with it, but none as dubious as those who would come to surround its unacknowledged Scottish sister, under the chairmanship of her good friend John Finlay Stewart. Kitty Atholl's silence on the Scottish League for European Freedom is eloquent.

Chapter Five

Spies in the City

The Scottish League for European Freedom never wanted for money, opening its doors for business, as it were, in 1945, in plush offices on George Street at the heart of Edinburgh's financial and commercial hub. Its chairman, John Finlay Stewart, invariably clad in Stewart tartan Highland dress, lunched with the good and the great of Edinburgh's New Town – the lawyers, the bankers, the stockbrokers and the newspaper editors of Scotland's capital city. He must have derived much quiet satisfaction from his social standing in this most class conscious of Scottish cities, for his origins were humble indeed.

He was born in 1871 in a tenement flat on Leven Street, close to the King's Theatre. He was the son of a domestic servant, circumstances he kept very much to himself in his new incarnation as a citizen of Edinburgh. Some time in the following ten years the family emigrated to South Africa. They prospered, and in 1889 he was a civil servant in the government of the Cape of Good Hope. Intriguingly, in Stewart's obituary, his friend George Waters, a former *Scotsman* editor, wrote of him that 'he served under President Kruger in the Transvaal', implying that Stewart fought with the Boers against the British. The Transvaal theatre of the war was one in which the Boers relied heavily on guerrilla and covert actions, and would have been a veritable university in the very darkest arts of espionage.

Stewart clearly had a sharp intellect. He qualified as an engineer and was an accomplished linguist. He was fluent in German, French, Spanish, Italian, Portuguese and, of course, in Afrikaans. He could also get by in Russian, Polish and Ukrainian. As an engineering consultant he travelled the world, but always described himself as a South African Scot. He spoke with a Scots accent, which was surely an affectation, as he had left the country before he was ten, and until the late 1930s spent most of his time abroad. One gets the impression that his accent and his habitual kilt wearing were part of a carefully cultivated image of Scottishness. His rhetoric often drew parallels between the historical struggles of the small nation of Scotland and the post-war struggles of the small nations of eastern Europe.

It was an image that certainly appealed to one of his most important levers into Edinburgh society and most significant contacts for ensuring good media coverage, George Waters. This former editor of the *Scotsman*, a short stocky man with thick spectacles, had been born in Thurso and brought up in a strict Calvinist household. This did not stop him enjoying a long lunch, or his habit of going home every evening for dinner and returning to the office to oversee putting the paper to bed. 'A benevolent authoritarian, at times a severe man, but tempered by an old world paternalism', was how he was described by one of his staff. the *Scotsman*, with the exception of the government propaganda sheet and the *Communist Daily Worker* was the only newspaper printed during the General Strike. Waters had no time for trade unionism.

He was an early proponent of Scottish devolution. In September 1932, at the time of the emerging Scottish National Party, a Scottish Home Rule Movement was launched, proposing a devolved settlement. It was founded by the likes of the Duke of Montrose, the Marquis of Douglas and 'a good showing of knights and baronets'. Its central philosophy was summed up by the duke: 'We believe that with a parliament of our own, we could, and would, manage our own affairs better than they are being managed from Westminster today. By relieving Westminster we could strengthen its hands to deal with the vital foreign questions with which it is now faced.'

Waters, who was present at that meeting, began writing leaders in the *Scotsman* broadly backing the case for a Scottish parliament. The idea of devolution horrified the Glasgow business community, who began a vigorous campaign against the idea. Their cause was taken up by the *Glasgow Herald*, and not for the first and certainly not for the last time, Scotland's two great home-grown broadsheets lobbed intellectual grenades at one another.

The core of this argument would rumble on for more than sixty years. The *Herald* was convinced 'that the interests of England and Scotland are are so interwoven, and the ramifications of trade so intricate, that Home Rule for Scotland would be altogether contrary to the interests of the country'. Waters countered with a leader titled with heavy sarcasm: 'Down on your knees, Scotland, and thank England for the benefits she has conferred on us.' It made the case for devolution as a liberating force for both the economy, and what he described as the best way Scotland could 'realise her own soul . . . Scotland would acquire a larger and freer life, that, less in the shadow of her dominating neighbour, she would experience a spiritual, and possibly also an economic rebirth.' This is familiar stuff to anyone acquainted with the arguments which dominated Scottish politics for a generation. Waters even suggested a constitutional convention: 'If men of goodwill get together would it not be possible to devise a constitution for Scotland that would work smoothly and without friction?'

The appeal of the SLEF to Waters was clearly its propaganda line of small nations being subjugated by the Soviet Union. The former *Scotsman* editor often spoke on behalf of the League and his most frequent theme was to draw parallels between the likes of Latvia or the Ukraine and the long Scottish struggle to maintain its identity in the shadow of a larger neighbour. This theme had a resonance in Scotland, something Stewart and Kitty Atholl would have been well aware of. It was a major factor in providing a good turnout at public meetings, and in the membership of the chairman of the Scottish National Party, Professor Andrew Gibb. Waters was an important figure for the League to have on board, becoming, in effect, its press officer. He ensured good media coverage for the SLEF, but also managed to influence the reporting of east European affairs in the *Scotsman* and its sister paper, the *Edinburgh Evening Despatch*.

Other characters, however, came with less savoury intellectual backgrounds. Major General John Fredrick Charles Fuller, was a close confidant of Stewart's, had been a member of Archibald Maul Ramsay's pro-Nazi Nordic League and Right Club. He had been close to Mosley in the 1930s, so close, it was said that he would have been Minister of Defence if the Fascists had ever formed a government. Known to his friends as 'Boney', he was a little man with a bald head, a sharp face and a nose of Napoleonic cast, whose frequent attacks on the army hierarchy were described by a comrade as 'viewed in the spirit of a rat hunt, a spirit he responded to with much vivacity and not a little wit'. In military terms Fuller had, during the First World War, been a moderniser, frustrated in the 1920s by a hidebound high command.

Not to put too fine a point on it, Fuller invented the idea of the Blitzkrieg, later refined in theory by Basil Liddell Hart and General de Gaulle and in practice by the Wehrmacht. He was largely responsible for the successful use of massed tanks at the Battle of Cambrai in 1917, a success largely thrown away by his superiors' failure to take advantage of the breakthrough. He developed 'Plan 1919' for the deployment of fast tanks with a range of 200 miles attacking in mass and in depth with air support, a plan shelved by the army post-1918. In 1919 he won the gold medal of the Royal United Services Institute for an essay in which he set out a blueprint for a reformed army based on mechanisation and the technical development of aircraft, wireless and gas. He also gained no mean reputation as a military historian, his magnum opus being the three volume, *Decisive Battles of the Western World*.

Freed of military office in the 1930s, Fuller became involved with the less savoury intellectual life of the time. He dabbled in the occult, and was a frequent visitor to the Loch Ness-side home of his friend Aleister Crowley, the 'Beast'. He spent some months in 1935–36 with Mussolini's forces in Abyssinia, seeing at first hand how effective modern poison gas could be in combination with mechanised infantry and tanks. In April 1939 he was a guest at Hitler's birthday celebrations in Berlin. He wrote reports for the Führer's propaganda minister Joseph Goebbels on British organisations and on individuals of interest to the Nazis. His speciality in his public speeches as a Ramsay acolyte was anti-Semitism, of the Jewish–Bolshevik plot variety and strongly pro-Nazi. Herein lies the central mystery of Fuller. He was not arrested along with the other leading members of the Right Club and Mosley's fascists in May 1940.

Indeed, Fuller attended the last meeting of a pro-Nazi group in May 1940, the day after the first wave of arrests. Under the cover of the Information and Policy Group, Right Club members had been meeting since the outbreak of war on the pretext of discussing agricultural matters. the *Daily Telegraph* managed to get a journalist into this final meeting, and he reported that news of the arrests caused alarm amongst the forty or so people there, and several of the members, including Fuller, left immediately. The *Evening Standard* followed up the story and he told them: 'I understood were were going to have a talk on egg farming and found that someone else was going to lecture.' He claimed he had once contributed a paper on economic warfare, and denied all knowledge of people he had been meeting in pro-Nazi circles for a decade. Fuller wasn't even interviewed by Special Branch, let alone, like many lesser members, cautioned, in spite of the fact that he had been under MI5 surveillance. The most likely explanation is that he was, in fact, an MI6 agent.

This brings us back to the Intermarium and the Bandera connection. Fuller had helped German Intelligence penetrate Ukrainian émigré groups in London in the 1930s. This was not, from the MI6 point of view at the time, as bizarre an act as it seems at first sight. As we have seen, at this period the Abwehr and MI6 were both involved in espionage operations on the ground involving Bandera's Organisation of Ukrainian

Nationalists and, if not acting exactly hand in glove, they were pursuing the same objective, namely, Soviet destabilisation. With another friend of Kitty Atholl's, the Labour MP Richard Stokes, Fuller managed to assist Yaroslav Stetzko, Bandera's lieutenant, wanted as a war criminal by Moscow, escape to the UK. Fuller was key to the SLEF operation as the link to Ukrainians being held in displaced persons camps in Britain and in continental Europe, including former SS and police battalion members who had seen service with Stetzko during the Lviv pogrom.

Other prominent members brought dubious baggage along with their anti-Communism. The first president was the Earl of Mansfield, who had been active in the British Empire Union and had been a founder of the Imperial Policy Group, a pro-appeasment and anti-Bolshevik think tank whose secretary, Kenneth de Courcy, was, interestingly, a friend and frequent luncheon companion of MI6 chief Stewart Menzies. Lt-Colonel Sir Thomas Moore, the Tory MP for Ayr Burghs, was a one-time admirer of Hitler, and an anti-Bolshevik whose views were hardened by service in the British army during the intervention in support of the White Russians from 1918 to 1920. Although he briefly supported Mosley, he was more a naively deluded fan of the glittering facade of Nazi Germany in general and its Führer in particular. A member of the Anglo–German Fellowship, he wrote in its journal in 1937 that the British public was 'too apt to dwell on the treatment of the Jews and on the trouble with the churches, both equally regrettable, I admit', forgetting, as he put it, 'the enormous social progress in housing, roads, education and public health'. Another Unionist MP, Guy Lloyd, had worked with MI6 during the war. He had opposed the Yalta agreement, and was an important parliamentary link for the League in campaigning against the forcible repatriation of citizens of the USSR, many of whom were war criminals.

Otherwise, the governing body of the League consisted of people who were duped into believing its work was solely humanitarian and just. Sir David Moncrieff was moved by the plight of refugees and by a genuine revulsion at the humanitarian crimes perpetrated by the Soviet Union, as was a former governor of South Australia, Sir Malcolm Harvey.

Stewart worked for MI6 during the 1920s and 1930s when he was a consultant in the Baltic timber trade. In a letter to the Foreign Office he described himself as one 'who has seen much of Soviet Russia off the beaten track, and who for years up to the outbreak of war was, for business reasons, in the border countries for a considerable time each year', and who 'knew all the leaders of independence movements of non-Russian peoples inside the USSR'.

The Baltic states were of strategic importance in pre-Second World war espionage aimed at the Soviet Union. Directed from the MI6 station in Helsinki by Chief of Operations Harry Carr, agents within the Soviet Union were run by officers disguised as passport officials. The other key front was the Baltic timber trade. Carr himself had a background in the industry, as his family had owned timber mills in St Petersburg. Come the revolution the mills were nationalised and his family were forced to flee the newly-born Soviet Union. According to Tom Bower, who had unrivalled access to agents of the period, Carr was 'obsessively secretive', and for him 'security became an end in itself', to the extent that it marred his judgement and much of his intelligence material came from 'completely open sources', or had been 'manufactured'.

The main timber dealer in the capital of Estonia, Tallinn, was Sandy McKibben, an MI6 officer who had been born in pre-revolutionary Moscow of wealthy Scottish parents. One of his main sources was the Estonian Director of Military Intelligence, Colonel Villen Saarsen. Unfortunately for MI6, as was so often the case in 1930s eastern Europe, Saarsen was also dealing with the Abwehr. It is likely that Stewart's role, with a cover that would allow him access to remote forest border regions, would have been to run agents in Russia, liaise with dissident groups, and with the leaders of his 'independence movements of non-Russian peoples'. His was no deskbound intelligence work but the sharp end of the business, where throats can get slit and interrogation is just another name for torture. Bower's assessment of the pre-war Baltic operation, however, was that it was 'amateurish in the extreme'.

During the time of the Nazi–Soviet pact, in June 1940, the USSR invaded the Baltic states. In common with Poland and Ukraine, these three nations – Estonia, Latvia and Lithuania – had endured a long history of being squeezed between German and Russian aspirations. Yet in the 1930s they were not havens of peace and democracy. Many Balts were enthusiastic about Nazi policy, particularly racial policy. When the Nazis invaded the Soviet Union they found ready allies in the Baltic.

At the Wannsee Conference, the meeting in January 1942 in a Berlin lakeside villa that decided on the 'final solution', Reinhard Heydrich asked that most conscientious of bureaucrats, Adolf Eichmann, for statistics for the number of Jews in Europe. When he reached Estonia on his list he announced it was already 'Jew-free', in the charming Nazi expression of the time. 'Do you know,' quipped Heydrich, 'that's the only good thing I have ever heard about Estonia.' Eichmann was also able to announce that in Lithuania only 34,000 of the 130,000 Jews who had been living there in July 1941 were still alive.

These killings were not carried out by the SS and by Einsatzgruppen alone, they were aided by local paramilitary units raised to root out and execute Jews, gypsies and Communists and to execute or deport them to the gas chambers. In Latvia the special battalion responsible for executing and deporting Jews was organised by Lt-Colonel Robert Osis, Director of Operations in the puppet government's Ministry of the Interior. Osis had been recruited before the war by MI6. Many of the killings took place on ground which would have been familiar to John Finlay Stewart, the Rumbula Forest. Yet, as we shall see, the Balts became favoured immigrants to the UK after the war.

Now confined to Stockholm, MI6 struggled to maintain contact with the Baltic states. According to Tom Bower, they even took quite a time to get their heads round the idea that the world had changed and the enemy was now Nazi Germany and not the Soviet Union. Only one agent was sent into the Baltic during the war, Ronald Seth, on what proved to be a botched mission in Estonia. Before the war Seth was Professor of English at Tallinn University, and associate editor of the *Baltic Times*. He wrote a book on the country, '*Baltic Corner. Travels in Estonia*', a fascinating glimpse of a strange world where ancient myths and fertility rituals merged with Christianity in the countryside, yet where, in the capital, chess was played in coffee shops and the symphonies of Brahms were discussed at dinner parties. In 1939 when news came of the pact with Nazi Germany, he fled to Newcastle. Given the nest of British spies that were in the Estonian capital it is perfectly possible he was already involved in Intelligence work.

His self-serving volume on his 1942 mission, *A Spy has no Friends*, tells us that he had worked out a plan to knock out the Estonian mining industry, sent a copy to 'intelligence' and was seconded from the RAF to the Special Operations Executive. An SOE Major told him that even if his plan was successful his chances of survival were estimated to be 15 per cent. The operation was given the strange but entirely appropriate title of Blunderhead.

Seth was spotted by a Nazi patrol as he landed, lost most of his equipment in making his escape, and went on the run. His story speaks volumes on Estonian attitudes at the time. He found it difficult to get help: 'I had lost everything, and found little local co-operation.' Starving, he managed to reach a friend after twelve days living rough. He was then mistaken by a mob for a 'filthy Russian' and fell into the hands of the Gestapo.

Beyond this point Seth's memoir has much to be self-serving about. He survived only by deserting to the Nazi cause, which he claimed was a ruse. 'I knew,' he wrote, 'that the information I had collected regarding codes, contacts and operations of German Intelligence would still be valuable . . . the idea of getting myself home to England began to suggest itself.' He was placed in a POW camp as a spy for the Nazis, and claimed his reports on inmates were 'distorted' to give false impressions of morale and opinions on the war. He then asserted that he duped Himmler into believing that he was a more important agent than he was, and that the SS leader appointed him as an envoy to deliver a peace plan to Churchill, proposing that the Western Allies combine with Germany to 'destroy the

Bolshevik menace'. Seth did reach Switzerland and in many quarters his story was treated with a deal of scepticism.

One Estonian contact of Stewart's did have a record untainted by Nazi dealings: Ants Oras, the Professor of English at Tartu University. This mild-mannered, chess-playing expert on the poetry of his native country was also a courageous man of action. Not all Estonians were happy to collaborate with the Nazis, and Oras was one of the leaders of the, albeit small, resistance movement attacking the Germans and their puppets. He ran boats between Sweden and Estonia carrying weapons, supplies and intelligence couriers. When the Soviets re-occupied the country he ran the gauntlet of the Russian navy, using his small boats to get people out of the Baltic states and away from the clutches of the secret police. This was the operation Kitty Atholl learned about from the 'Latvian Min-ister' enjoying the fishing in Birnham.

Oras was the Estonian representative at the first of the international gatherings in Edinburgh organised by the Intermarium network through the Scottish League for European Freedom. The importance placed by the Soviets on such a gathering, particularly if it involved Estonia, Latvia and Lithuania, can be judged by a GCHQ intercept of late 1945. From 'Viktor' in Moscow to 'Igor' in the London embassy, it reports that information has been received 'that a Conference of representatives of emigrants from the Baltic States is to be held', and requests that he 'reports URGENTLY what you think'. 'Viktor' was the codename for Lt-General P.M. Fitin of Soviet intelligence, and Igor was the codename for Konstantin Kuken, the counsellor at the embassy handling Polish and Baltic affairs.

The Edinburgh Congress of the Oppressed European

Spies in the City

Nations opened in Rainy Hall on 25 June 1946. The opening meeting was chaired by George Waters, who began his speech with his usual resounding rhetoric on small nations and the cosmopolitan nature of the average Scot, before moving on to the unfolding east European situation. 'There could be little doubt,' he told the Congress, 'that the ultimate intention of Moscow was to create a solid political, economic and military bloc in eastern Europe subservient to herself,' which was a precise analysis of what was indeed happening. August Zaleski, chairman of the Central European Federal Clubs, gave the opening delegate speech, a long dissertation on the benefits of a federal system in central and eastern Europe, ending with what was to be something of a recurring theme. Western culture and Christianity. 'Those nations,' he said, 'are proud to be of the Christian faith, and Western civilisation.' This religious strand at the conference is hardly surprising as the Vatican were at this stage providing some of the funding and some of the ideological input for Intermarium. The mute ghosts at the feast came from the empty ghettos of eastern Europe.

When the Latvian delegate, the Rev. Roberts Slokenbergs rose to speak, the air became heavy with the scent of hypocrisy. 'On September 1st 1939,' he claimed, 'when Germany attacked our neighbour, Poland, we could see anew how anti-German our nation was.' This would be the anti-German Latvia that provided the Kommando units who murdered 29,000 Jews in the Rumbula Forest, the Schutzpolizei to guard the Riga ghetto and the SS unit who rounded up Jews in the Warsaw ghetto and dispatched them on the trains to the Treblinka death camp. The Rev. Slokenbergs may well have been innocent of any active participation in what really

97

happened in Latvia during the Nazi occupation, but he was certainly guilty of joining in the great Baltic conspiracy of post-war silence. He was also an MI6 asset. He visited the UK in 1944 via the service's Stockholm office. The file on this visit remains closed.

The Slovakian delegate, however, had been an active participant in the Nazi cause. Peter Pridavok spoke eloquently of the Stalinisation of his country, and its cultural impact: 'Today education has been replaced by political indoctrination and militarism, and if this continues the whole of our distinctive Slovakian culture will disappear within a few years.' According to a Foreign Office file, Pridavok was 'one-time editor of the *Slovak*, the official organ of Hlinka Slovak People's Party, later chief of the Slovak Press Bureau'.

The party had been founded by a Catholic cleric, Monsignor Andrej Hlinka. It was a nationalist party which sought the break-up of Czechoslovakia and the founding of an independent Slovakian state. Beyond that, it adopted an increasingly extreme neo-Nazi and anti-Semitic programme during the 1930s. When Hlinka died in 1938 he was replaced by Monsignor Jozef Tiso, and in the wake of the Munich agreement, with the help of Berlin, they seized their chance and established a neo-Nazi Slovakia in March 1939. There was never any need for the SS to become involved in racial policies here. They had their own version, the Hlinka Guard, and their own race laws. They began exterminating the Slovakian Jewish population in September 1941. This was the state for which Pridavok had been chief spin doctor.

The architect of Slovakian race policy was the Foreign Minister, Dr Ferdinand Durcansky, another Intermarium and MI6 asset. He had been condemned by the Czech government as a war criminal, a verdict recognised by the UN, and had evaded capture with the aid of British Intelligence and the Vatican. He did not attend the 1946 Edinburgh congress but sent a fraternal message from his lair in Rome: 'The Slovak Action Committee is sending greetings with wishes of full success to the Congress of Oppressed European Nations. The Slovak nation is already fighting for its liberation and wishes cooperation in this fight and in the creation of a Central European Confederation.'

Of course it was not the public speeches of the delegates that mattered so much as the work that went on in the background. In 1946 Czechoslovakia was at a crossroads. After the Nazi occupation a provisional government was set up by the exiled president, Edvard Beneš, first in Paris, then in London. He signed an alliance with the Soviet Union in 1943, and became the only émigré leader allowed by Stalin to return to his country after the war. Free multi-party elections were held in 1946 and the Communists polled 40 per cent of the vote, and held key posts in the government formed after the poll. In the event, Beneš' belief that he could work with Stalin in a spirit of realpolitik inevitably proved hollow. Popular support for the Communists waned as events in the rest of the region unfolded, and they seized power with the help of the Red Army in 1948. In 1946, however, it seemed to the West as if there was a chance Stalin could be thwarted in at least one east European state by genuine free elections and in the Kremlin there was the prospect of a propaganda coup in the shape of a Communist victory without resorting to dirty tricks, terrorism or tanks.

British Intelligence were taking the pessimistic view and banking on a Stalinist Czechoslovakia, which, of course, was to be the ultimate outcome. Hence, in Edinburgh, they retained the potentially destabilising Slovak card, and from the Czech side they brought on board a long-time opponent of President Beneš, General Lev Prchala. He had fled to Poland after the Nazi occupation of Czechoslovakia, organised an escape route from Prague to Warsaw and managed to form a small military unit to fight alongside the Poles in 1939. After the fall of Poland he fled to France, and arrived in the UK at the same time as Edvard Beneš.

Prchala opposed Beneš and his close relationship with the Soviets. Prchala formed the Czech National Committee, which refused to recognise the legitimacy of the provisional government. According to a Foreign Office report: 'This group maintained contact with reactionary Polish circles and toyed with the idea of a Central European Federal Union . . . General Prachala and his friends are certainly strongly anti-Communist and anti-Soviet.' In January 1946 the British Ambassador in Prague reported that the Czech government were claiming Prchala was organising 'diversionary activities from the safety of Great Britain'. The Foreign Office thought it unlikely there was any foundation for these allegations and that the Prague embassy was 'satisfied that the propaganda campaign was a Communist ramp and an ill-conceived one at that . . . despite reports that the Czech government had resolved to request General Prchala's extradition, no such request has yet been received by the Foreign Office.'

The question arises as to why MI6 were talent-spotting as potential agents for covert operations quite so many people with Nazi baggage. The answer is relatively simple: by definition, these were the very people who had experience of covert action against the Soviet Union when they threw their lot in with Berlin. Yet that begs a further question: there is surely a moral difference between misguidedly 'throwing your lot in', and the likes of Pridavok and Durcansky, who were actually Nazis.

Not that this was new territory for British Intelligence. It was MI6 who first covertly enlisted General Reinhard Gehlen, the head of Wehrmacht intelligence on the Eastern Front. He was passed on to US Intelligence, not because of moral scruples, but because there were not the financial resources to handle the wealth of material in Gehlen's hands. MI6 also recruited Karl Marcus, who had run agents for the SS Sicherheitsdienst in Belorussia. He was appointed mayor of a small town in the British Zone; using this cover, he recruited former SS Intelligence officers with experience in the Ukraine who had links with Bandera's OUN. Interestingly, one of the recruits was a Dr Emil Hoffman, who belonged to Deutsche Revolution, a neo-Nazi group whose aim was to build a west European federation as an anti-Soviet bulwark.

The broader philosophical question is why so many central and east European states developed their own home-grown versions of Nazism. The answer is largely their deep-rooted Christian anti-Semitism. Peasant societies in 1930s Baltic states, Croatia, Slovakia and elsewhere had seen little social change since the Middle Ages and retained a pious medieval mindset. This was the anti-Semitism of the Jew as Christkiller, of Jew as the abductor and torturer of Christian children, of Jew as desecrator of the host and the poisoner who brought disease to the God-fearing peasant. In 1267, for example, the Council of Vienna banned the purchase of meat from Jewish butchers on the grounds that it was likely to be poisoned. In the fourteenth century there was a Europe-wide belief that the Jews had poisoned the wells and caused the Black Death. That unleashed a pogrom from the Atlantic to the Urals, in all but one country. Sixty large, and more than 150 smaller communities were exterminated, and 350 massacres short of outright extermination took place. The one exception was Poland, where King Casimir, probably influenced by his Jewish mistress, gave the Jews of Europe sanctuary. It is a terrible comment on the history of our continent that some 600 years later the spiritual inheritors of the clerical anti-Semites arrived and all but wiped out their descendants.

Norman Cohn, in his *Pursuit of the Millennium*, has drawn revealing parallels between Christian anti-Semitism and the roots of Nazism. The 1 May 1934 edition of the Nazi magazine, *Der Stürmer*, is devoted to the alleged murders of Christian children, with copious illustrations of rabbis sucking blood from Aryan children, images straight from the nightmare pulpits of the fourteenth century. In peasant societies the image of the exploitative Jewish merchant was a powerful one, and it remained the subject of a deal of popular German literature in the nineteenth century. Hitler, himself the product of small-town rural Austria, claimed the novel *Der Buettner Baner* by Wilhelm von Polenz (1895) had 'opened my eyes to the racial question'. Typically for the genre, a merchant, without character or roots, descends from the city and swindles the honest and virtuous German peasant. In the final scene the peasant, overlooking his former fields where the Jew is building a factory, hangs himself. It plays on two fears: one racial, one the abiding mistrust of countryside for the metropolitan and industrial. These ideas had wide currency throughout central and eastern Europe, and in hard times resonated loudly and bleakly, turning Jewish communities into easy scapegoats.

The other question raised is how MI6 was to pay for their plan to launch special operations around the Soviet Union and eastern Europe. On the local level, Stewart's daughter later said she 'often wondered about a Ukrainian go-between who used to turn up with a different name each time' and about how it was the Scottish League for European Freedom was so affluent. Stephen Dorril, in *MI6: Fifty Years of Special Operations*, also intriguingly speculates on how the whole MI6 service was funded after the war. This was the age of austerity, of make-do and mend, of queues outside food shops, of rationing, of a fuel crises in the midst of the worst winters in living memory. The cash allocated by parliament to fund MI6 was small, and, aside from eastern Europe, there were large-scale operations in the Middle East. It is true that in defence matters the Attlee government were adept at creative accounting, and managed, for example, to disguise the funding of Britain's atomic bomb programme by spreading it around a number of budgets. Dorril suggests that British Intelligence used Operation Safehaven funds, 'which originated with the gold hoard that the Germans plundered from Europe . . . A knowledgeable insider source has suggested that a portion of this tainted gold was, indeed, used by MI6 to fund its special operations.'

Safehaven went beyond simply the disposal of Nazi loot. In a memo from the Economic Warfare Division in 1945 its first objective was defined as, 'an attempt to locate, immobilise and facilitate the disposition of enemy assets,' making it clear that assets are 'defined in their widest connotation'. This would appear to include, in the words of one note from an official, 'obnoxious Germans who we propose to repatriate from overseas'.

There is an allegation that Safehaven was also used by American Intelligence to fund operations in Italy, though this is denied by the CIA. What is clear is that there was a degree of creativity on the part of the US in their definition of the 'widest connotation' of the word 'asset' in their pursuit of self interest, outlined in another 1945 British report on Safehaven: 'The Americans represent some classes of German, varying from professors and technologists to propagandists as constituting a kind of "intellectual asset" analogous to economic assets which we want to deny to the Germans. It is fairly evident the Americans are also deeply interested in removing any kind of commercial competition. It does not go without saying that the elimination of competition is in British interests.'

The first operation, in the Baltic, was a botched omen of things to come. Stewart's old comrade from Tallinn days, Sandy McKibben, and his boss, Harry Carr, working from their Stockholm base, planned to reactivate contact with the Latvian underground, who were conducting a bitter guerrilla war from bases deep in the forests. They decided that, rather than air drops, they would use the method tried and tested by Professor Ants Oras, fast motor boats across the Baltic. Carried out in conjunction with Swedish Intelligence, the operation was launched in August 1946. It had to be abandoned when the boat carrying the mission's weapons and supplies capsized in a freak storm.

This, of course, was simply plain bad luck. Their next operation went awry for altogether more sinister reasons. It was to be, in the jargon of the Intelligence world, a 'false flag' ploy. Not to put too fine a point on it, MI6 made it look like a US operation by using American equipment and weapons. In early 1947 three agents were landed on the Latvian coast; almost immediately they fell into the hands of Soviet Intelligence, and were subjected to sustained interrogation. It should have been blindingly obvious that the speed of their capture indicated that something was sorely amiss and that somewhere along the line security was compromised. Crucially, their radio had been captured intact and this was to prove a devastating blow to the Latvian underground.

August Bergmanis was a radio operator and former resistance fighter who had been tortured and recruited by the Soviets. In March he used the captured radio to inform Stockholm that all was well. In August a fishing boat landed two further agents. They were kept under surveillance and made contact with Bergmanis. A meeting was arranged with underground leaders in Riga, and they discussed plans, tactics and further contacts with the two genuine agents and Bergmanis. As a result, by the end of the year most of the leading figures in the Latvian underground had been killed or captured.

This did not deter MI6, and even when mission after mission failed, it did not seem to occur to anyone in the organisation that something was seriously amiss internally.

Chapter Six

Westward Ho

At the end of the war about one in eight of those wearing a German uniform were citizens of the Soviet Union. In Europe, seven million people were on the move in all directions. As the poet Gottfried Benn put it, 'We trudged over icy highways clogged up with endless rows of refugees in covered wagons from which dead children fell.' In Germany there were 8,000,000 foreign workers, 175,000 were Balts, 1,000,000 were Polish, 3,000,000 were designated as being citizens of the USSR, 285,000 of whom were from ethnic minorities who denied that citizenship and were to refuse repatriation. Almost 125,000 Ukrainians, Caucasians and White Russians and a further 20,000 Balts had left their homes in the Soviet Union and come to Germany as the Red Army advanced. Hiding amongst liberated slave labourers were untold numbers of collaborators, former camp guards and paramilitaries. Beyond the ruins of the Reich were many millions more; all were, in the expression of the time, displaced persons, or DPs.

There were also the prisoners of war. At Yalta Britain had agreed to send back all Soviet citizens who were within the British zones of occupation. Between May and September 1945 over 2,000,000 went more or less willingly, but then the forcible repatriations of the ethnic minorities who had chosen to side with the Germans began. There were great and there were small brutalities.

In October 1945 an agent reported on the 'Behaviour of Red Army Soldiers at Detmold in the British Occupied Zone'. A fifteen-year-old high school student, Orest Pobihushka, was heading into the town centre. On a street corner Soviet soldiers, with the help of 'several civilians', were stopping passers-by they suspected of not being German nationals, and demanding to examine their documents. One of the Red Army soldiers approached the boy and and shouted, 'Papiere zeigen!' Pobihushka produced his Polish registration certificate. The soldier wasn't satisfied and demanded other documents and, without waiting for a reply, unbuttoned the boy's coat and extracted a Red Cross certificate. 'So, you are a Ukrainian,' and with these words seized him by the collar, kicked him, and threw him into a truck already occupied by a number of people who had been seized in a similar manner. In a few moments the vehicle was full and drove off, but as the truck ascended a hill Pobihushka jumped out and escaped. The agent noted the reaction of British soldiers watching the round-up: 'To the pleadings of the student, "I will not go to Russia, I am Ukrainian and have never lived in Russia", an English soldier answered, "I am only standing here and watching", and without a word or act in the defence of the student looked on upon the Soviet acts of violence. It seemed as if he was in conspiracy with the Red Army soldiers in capturing innocent people.'

The United Nations Relief and Rehabilitation Administration, UNRRA, protested about US army behaviour at a Ukrainian DP camp, Redouten Saale. At eleven o'clock on the night of 30 July 1945, an armed American guard was thrown around the camp. Suspicions were allayed when the officer in charge, a Major Cilley, told the inmates they were being transported to Hanover in the British Zone to work. According to the UNRRA report: 'Some were glad, for reasons of personal security, to be escaping from the US zone.'

In the early hours of the morning the Americans locked the camp and the truth arrived in the shape of Soviet trucks. The refugees were then ordered, under guard, to get on board. 'Some did so under compulsion,' UNRRA reported, 'others, en route, cut their way out of the covered roofs and fell off as best they could when the trucks were travelling. Others jumped off, and, if uninjured, ran into town. Most of them left without baggage because they were so terrified.'

At another camp US soldiers helped the Soviets forcibly repatriate Ukrainian women and children; given the reputation of the Red Army for rape, one can imagine the fate awaiting many. Attracted by their screams, 'a mass of people gathered', and the troops panicked. 'One young American officer,' UNRRA recorded, 'was particularly brutal; armed with a pistol, he violently swung a heavy cane in all directions. He struck the people as if they were a herd of cattle. A soldier fired in the air. The crowd shrieked in panic.' One man, who tried to run away, 'received tons of blows from rifle butts, helmets, bats and fists on his head, chest, back and face, until, finally, the soldiers carried him away to the camp prison. His wife fell to the ground, stricken with a heart attack.'

The Red Army trucks drove off. The fighting suddenly stopped. The 'whole camp shuddered at the screams of the women and the children'. The crowd jeered at the Americans, 'regarding their democratic talk and their undemocratic acts'.

To be fair, most troops, certainly most British troops,

loathed involvement in the repatriations. The considerable force used when thousands of Cossacks – men, women and children – were ordered out of their camp at Klagenfurt in the British Zone and into Soviet hands created a growing sense of unease amongst press, public and military in the UK. A British ship, *Empire Pride*, was used in one operation to take several hundred Cossacks to Odessa, and when they docked a group of about thirty was taken by Soviet Guards behind a dockside warehouse. A quarter of an hour later there was a burst of machine-gun fire. In spite of a growing body of evidence testifying that the fate of those being forced back to the Soviet Union was almost certain death, the Foreign Office was wary of provoking the Kremlin, and it wasn't until June 1946 that the Cabinet officially discontinued the policy of assisting in forced repatriation, seven months after the Americans.

There were two ironies here. The first was that Italy, under the control of Marshal Sir Harold Alexander, was a haven for war criminals, including a group of indubitably guilty Ukrainians, the entire Galizien SS division. The second, and it was to become linked to the first, was that for a year the British had followed a policy that swept up guilty and innocent, and were now to follow a policy in which the guilty were more often than not allowed sanctuary in the UK.

The British government came to see this seething mass of the dispossessed not so much as a humanitarian problem, more as the solution to a domestic economic problem, the manpower gap, as it was called. The government's economic survey for 1947 almost casually introduced the new policy designed to plug this gap: 'Foreign labour can make a useful contribution to our needs . . . The Government intends to extend the recruitment of displaced persons from the continent to work here.' In March, in the shadow of a fuel crisis, the Chancellor, Stafford Cripps, told the Commons he hoped there would be 100,000 foreigners at work in the UK by the end of the year. It was even suggested that a solution to language difficulties could be overcome by sinking special pits to be completely staffed by former refugees.

There had been a precedent of a kind: the Balt Cygnet scheme, a suggestion first mooted at a meeting between officials of the Ministries of Labour and Health in 1945. There had been an extreme shortage of domestic staff in hospitals, particularly sanatoria, throughout the war, and improvements in pay and conditions in 1945 had done nothing to alleviate what one official described as 'a crisis'. The scheme was to recruit young women from the Baltic states to fill the vacant posts. It must be stressed that this was no attempt to get labour at below the going rate; they were employed with exactly the same pay and conditions as their British counterparts. The first recruits arrived in April 1947, and within two months some eleven and a half thousand had arrived. Why Balts? The answer is that in the opinion of the Foreign Office they were considered to be 'better types than the Poles'.

The philosophy which was to imbue the larger scheme for industrial workers – codenamed Westward Ho – was set out by two left-wing think-tanks, the Fabian Society and PEP, Political and Economic Planning. In setting out the case for the need to import labour, PEP highlighted the Scottish situation, which was worse than the UK average: 'Between 1861 and 1938 the net loss through emigration was 1.4 million, compared with 1.8 million for England and Wales, with ten times the population.'

The Fabian Society document, *Population and the People*, is quite shocking to modern eyes, particularly so to anyone of a leftward persuasion. It begins by setting out the case for the kind of Socialist programme one would expect: family allowances, maternity benefits, and even talk of the need to allow women to balance career and family. It is when it moves on to consider the problem of the declining and ageing population that it enters territory which one would not today associate with left-wing or liberal thinking: 'Married couples, of healthy stock, should, whatever their social class, be encouraged to breed.'

When the Fabians turned to immigration, they produced rhetoric which would have been quite at home in the Third Reich: 'We need to encourage parents of healthy stock to settle in the British Isles, and to discourage those whom we already have from leaving.' The ideal was 'men and women of European stock, between the ages of twenty and thirty. They are the immigrants best suited to assist population policy. They will enter the country at an age when they should be both fertile and economically productive.' There was, in this search for Socialist perfection, no room for the disabled: 'The utmost care should, of course, be taken to admit only those mentally and physically sound . . . The Eugenics of immigration cannot be over stressed.' I am not suggesting that the Fabians were really proto-Nazis, but the document does highlight how, even after the war, ideas such as 'good European stock', excluding those deemed to be 'unsound' and the whole notion of eugenics remained in the common currency of political thought. Nazism wasn't some aberration that just arrived from nowhere in the head of a deeply dysfunctional former corporal and failed artist. Nazi philosophy had a history and tapped into ideas which were shared with other political movements whose self image was 'progressive'.

The Fabian Society paper, whose views on immigration became the basis of government policy in Westward Ho, tuned in perfectly with MI6 aspirations to broaden the base of talent-spotting amongst east European refugees, and with the attitudes of the Civil Servants who would run the scheme. The PEP paper was, if anything, more explicit in its eugenic programme, adopting the five criteria set out by the Eugenics Society:

1. Sound physical health and good physique
2. Intelligence
3. Social usefulness
4. Freedom from genetic taints; that is, from diseases and defects likely to be transmitted to children
5. Membership of a large, united and well-adjusted family, and fondness for children

The PEP report did not, of course, advocate what it described as 'the authoritarian methods adopted in Nazi Germany', which they believed not only violated principles of personal freedom, but were 'eugenically unsound'.

Practical pressure to get the scheme under way came from industry. Members of the Cotton Board, who visited Germany in 1946 to examine machinery, returned with the idea of meeting their shortage of 100,000 workers by recruiting from the displaced persons camps. They inspired the United Nations Relief and Rehabilitation Administration to make an approach to the British government and were told that it was as likely as the 'resettlement of the refugees on the mountains of the moon'.

What concentrated minds was the ferocious winter of 1946/ 47, which provoked a fuel crisis of epic proportions. There were warning signs in late 1946: factories on short-time working, intermittent power cuts, warnings from the electricity industry that they couldn't meet demand and that 'we are moving towards a national calamity'. The generating stations were pre-war and outdated, but, perhaps more importantly, not enough coal was being mined and distributed to meet the demands of domestic and industrial users. On 5 February 1947 an arctic blizzard hit Britain with 60-mph winds. The power cuts became long and total. Two million were thrown out of work as factories closed for want of power. The coal supplies that existed were cut off from the consumers by a paralysed transport system. Shops ran out of food and candles. Thousands of the old and sick died in unheated homes. The labour shortage had come home to roost.

In 1958 a Ministry of Labour civil servant, J.A. Tannahill, wrote an account of the Westward Ho scheme. His figures, gleaned from his own department, show that of the 74,500 people who were initially involved, almost 21,000, more than a third, were Ukrainian. The tiny Baltic states of Latvia, Lithuania and Estonia provided a further 21,000 men and women. 'The recruiters,' Tannahill wrote, 'concentrated on the Baltic and then on the Ukrainian communities . . . the first batch of recruits landed in the United Kingdom on 2 April 1947, and within two months, 11,500 had arrived.' Poles were 'not at first encouraged to offer themselves'.

The Foreign Office mandarin in charge of this policy was an A.W.H. Wilkinson, Wilkie Wilkinson to his friends. The possibility of using labour from Britain's still far-flung Empire did not even enter the frame, nor did the possibility of Jewish immigration. Wilkinson's attitude to the latter was summed up in a sneering memo written after the formation of the state of Israel: 'I gather Jewish Societies are building up funds to use the post-1950 US immigration quotas for DPs as a means of pushing Jews unfit for work in Palestine into the USA.' He viewed those unfit for work, the elderly, or orphans, as 'hard cases' and did not recognise the millions of Germans who had been expelled from their homes in Poland or the Sudetenland as refugees. To him, 'it would be undesirable to discriminate between distressed Germans who have fled from Stettin from British bombs, and another who had fled the same town from Russian or Polish bayonets or bludgeons'; they were a 'demographic problem of Western Europe'. To him the Balts were 'the elite of the refugee problem'.

The problem, from the point of view of MI6, was screening. Too many Balts, particularly those the service would be interested in, had Nazi backgrounds that would not bear scrutiny. Kitty Atholl, under the banner of the British League for European Freedom, helped organise a powerful pro-Balt lobby in the House of Commons.

In late 1944 Elma Dangerfield assembled the duchess and four right-wing Tory MPs – Maurice Petherick, John Stourton, Major Guy Lloyd and Victor Raikes – at her home, and they agreed to set up the British League. Raikes was involved with Dangerfield on the Deportees Committee, an offshoot of the Middle Zone Association which she had set up with sometime MI6 agent, F.A. Voigt. Raikes was described by George Orwell as 'an able and outspoken reactionary'. Orwell attended the League's first public meeting, which he reported in *Tribune* as being attended by 'quite a large audience'. He wrote that he had met a journalist there, 'whose contacts with influential people are much more extensive than mine', who had told Orwell that he believed British foreign policy was about to take a violent anti-Russian swing and 'it would be quite easy to manipulate public opinion in that direction if necessary'.

One of those on the platform was Richard Stokes, a Labour MP who was proving a valuable ally in the matters of Baltic and Ukrainian immigration. Stokes was a champagne Socialist of the first rank, a millionaire businessman with extensive connections in the Middle East and the Intelligence world. He was one of the MPs who had worked to get Westward Ho off the ground, and was close to the MI6-sponsored Promethean League and to Intermarium. He was the friend of Major General 'Boney' Fuller, with whom he had successfully conspired to bring Yaroslav Stetzko to the UK. If not actually an MI6 agent, Stokes was effectively their spokesman on the floor of the House, and fixer within the governing party. In 1951 he was to lead the Stokes Mission to Tehran, accompanied by an MI6 agent, in an effort to make a dubious oil deal with Iran.

With Kitty Atholl's silence regarding the Scottish League and Elma Dangerfield telling the present author that she knew nothing of its existence, it is hard to tell what the relationship between the two organisations was, but it seems likely that they kept in touch through Stokes and Fuller, and the unacknowledged visits the duchess paid to her 'dear friend' John Finlay Stewart. The Leagues did coordinate the tone and timing of their propaganda efforts, and indeed one of Stewart's pamphlets, on the Baltic, carries the imprint of the 'Scottish Branch of the British League for European Freedom'. The Foreign Office certainly thought of them as working closely together. The FO like to keep what tabs they can on what their friends in MI6 are up to, and Wilkinson planted Frances Blackett in the BLEF's offices, working as honorary secretary. If, up in Edinburgh, Stewart should write or say anything the Foreign Office found alarming then Wilkinson would phone his informer for clarification.

There is, however, no sense in which the British League for European Freedom was the kind of hands-on MI6 front that its Scottish sister organisation was. There is evidence of funding from British Intelligence via Intermarium and the Poles, and Stephen Dorril has suggested that US money may have been involved. Its value was as a conduit to Parliament and a propaganda front. Two members were important for their media and Intelligence links. Edward Hulton, the publisher of *Picture Post* and founder, with F.A. Voigt, of the bogus Britanova News Agency, was on the advisory board. Tom Burns, Catholic publisher of *The Tablet*, who had worked for MI6 during the war, and as press attaché for the Ministry of Information in Spain had reported directly to Kim Philby, was a member and used his publication as a propaganda outlet.

The need for two Leagues becomes clear when one examines a propaganda strand of the BLEF which would have made it unacceptable to one of the main targets for assets in Edinburgh – the Ukrainians. In the late 1920s Kitty Atholl had befriended a White Russian émigré, Anatole Baykolov, whose book on Soviet repression, *In the Land of the Communist Dictatorship*, had profoundly influenced her view of events in Russia. Baykolov came to Britain after the Revolution in 1917 and made a living as a journalist. He was the chairman of the Russian Social Democrats in exile, and joined the British Labour Party. He was an adviser to the TUC on

Kitty, Duchess of Atholl: condemned by the left as 'The Fascist Beast' and by the right as 'The Red Duchess' (National Portrait Gallery, London)

Top. Elma Dangerfield. A former Intelligence officer turned journalist, she was the friend and fellow campaigner of the Duchess of Atholl. This photograph was taken when she was standing as a Liberal candidate for Aberdeen South in 1959. (Image courtesy of *The Herald* and *Evening Times* Picture Archive)

Below. Captain Archibald Maule Ramsay, the pro-Nazi Peebles MP who masterminded the deselection of the Duchess of Atholl (Trustees of the National Library of Scotland)

Top. John Finlay Stewart, Chairman of the Scottish League for European Freedom (Trustees of the National Library of Scotland)

Below. Delegates to the 1958 conference of the Anti-Bolshevik Bloc of Nations. Yaroslav Stetzko is second from the left in the front row. (Trustees of the National Library of Scotland)

Top. Stefan Bandera, the Ukrainian guerrilla leader (Trustees of the National Library of Scotland)

Below. This photograph, apparently showing Ukrainian partisans fighting the Red Army in the Carpathians, was actually faked by the Anti-Bolshevik Bloc of Nations in the Bavarian forest to deceive MI6 into believing there was a civil war raging in the Ukraine. (from Olev Martovych, *Ukrainian Liberation Movement in Modern Times*)

Top. Anton Gecas lived in quiet obscurity in an Edinburgh suburb until he was exposed in a 1987 television documentary as a member of a Lithuanian Police Battalion involved in the mass murder of Baltic and Russian Jews. He is pictured here at the Court of Session in 2001. (Image courtesy of *The Herald* and *Evening Times* Picture Archive)

Below. This photograph is thought to show Anton Gecas when he was a member of the Lithuanian Police Battalion

Top. Some members of the Galitzien Division taking a break at the Haddington camp in 1948 or 1949. The men had a reputation for being hard-working and knowledgeable farm hands. (courtesy of John Tully Jackson)

Below.The Galitzien Division camp orchestra (courtesy of John Tully Jackson)

Top. Ukrainian priests bless the 14th Waffen-SS
Galitzien Division colours (courtesy of John Tully Jackson)

Below. Ukrainian nationalism was a potent mix of religion,
ethnic pride and anti-semitism (courtesy of John Tully Jackson)

Soviet affairs and became close to the Bevinites in the trade union movement and the party's crusade against Communism.

In the 1930s, through Kitty Atholl, Baykolov became an advisor to Winston Churchill on the USSR, and later to the permanent under-secretary at the Foreign Office, Sir Robert Vansittart. This formidable anti-Communist mandarin ran his own Intelligence network, and recruited Baykolov as an agent. According to Kitty's biographer, S.J. Hetherington, Vansittart also recruited Kitty for a time when she took an interest in Nazi Germany, and she was fed information by the network's chief informant, Malcolm Christie. Baykolov was a supporter of the NTS (Narodnyi Trudovoy Soyuz, the National Labour Council), which had originally been set up in Belgrade in 1930 with the help of MI6 agent, Claudius Voss.

It was a 'Greater Russia' movement, which sought to destroy Soviet rule but to restore the boundaries of the Tsarist Empire. Baykolov's more covert work was to act as an informant for Captain Bob Kerby. Kerby was yet another agent with a forestry background, and espionage was in his blood. His father, a Scot, had been one of the Tsar's advisers on the timber industry, and one of MI6's first agents. According to Richard Deacon, a writer who met Bob Kerby shortly before his death, he was 'a huge man with a bald cannon-ball head and rubbery features usually creased with a smile for he had a lively sense of humour'. In the annals of British espionage the pairing of Baykolov and Kerby is famous, or infamous, for producing the accusation that Wallis Simpson, the paramour of the Prince of Wales, whose affair led to his abdication, was actually a German agent.

Baykolov was a major source of information for the British League for European Freedom, and for Elma Dangerfield in particular. From the point of view of MI6, having anti-Soviet Russians on board for their plans to destabilise the USSR was yet another arrow in the armoury, but their 'Greater Russia' stance would have been violently opposed by Ukrainians. Hence the logic of having two Leagues.

Dangerfield's journalistic enterprise, the *Whitehall News*, which had been purchased with the help of Polish funds, used Baykolov's material to good effect. It consistently reported on the development of Soviet weapons technology. In July 1947, two years before the first Soviet nuclear test, she reported on the growth of secret areas within the USSR, called in the piece 'Atomgrads'. One was 'in a mountain valley in the vicinity of the Black Sea . . . another, south-east of Omsk in an area now known as Little Germany on account of the number of German scientists working there. The third is under construction in Central Asia.' In March 1948 she reported on Bezimyanka, towns without names, 'built up under plans for colonising Soviet Central Asia and the Far East'. Later in the year she identified the sight of one 'Atomgrad' as being on the shores of Lake Baikal.

All of this is entirely accurate. We now know that in October 1946 a report was sent to Stalin detailing the special sites for nuclear research and that some 37,000 workers, most of them slaves, were involved. In 1948 GCHQ were ordered to make Soviet nuclear development their top priority. What is odd is that the West was so surprised when the first test took place in August 1949. All Western Intelligence services woefully underestimated the ability of Stalin to get the bomb, believing it couldn't be done before the mid-1950s at the earliest. To be fair, they didn't know that much essential material was being handed to the USSR in brown envelopes by Klaus Fuchs, the scientist of German extraction who had worked at Los Alamos and was on the team developing the British atomic bomb in the 1940s. He was convicted of spying in 1951.

A favourite theme of Dangerfield's was the exposure of Stalin's concentration camps. 'Until now,' she wrote in 1948, 'no one knew the Gulag administration maintained a slave labour colony in Franz Joseph Land, where the average temperature is 75 degrees below zero. Accommodation is provided in galleries of disused lead mines . . . 700 of the 1,000 inmates have died from an epidemic of dysentery and from lead poisoning.' She expanded Kitty Atholl's work on the Soviet occupation of Poland in 1939 and produced one of the earliest and best-sourced exposures of the Soviet slave empire in *Beyond the Urals*, which was published by the British League in 1948.

In 1947, however, the main thrust of the League's activities centred around the Balts, particularly the Latvians. They worked through the Society of Latvians, and the nation's ambassador in exile, Charles Zarine. They lobbied hard both in the Commons, largely through Stokes, and in the media. They developed a fiction that the Latvian Legion of the SS was purely a fighting unit, and most of its members had been compelled to join. Zarine wrote to the Foreign Office that: 'They were not fighting for Germany and the Nazi cause, but for the freedom of the Latvian people. At that time the primary danger was a repeated Russian invasion. The ultimate aim of all Latvian soldiers was to turn against the Germans at a later stage when the Russian danger had been avoided.' This of course, was nonsense. As we have seen, the Latvian SS evolved out of home-grown anti-Semitism, and in the matter of extermination they needed no lessons from Germany. As for compulsion, young Latvian males could have opted for units which were not SS. The 15th division of the Latvian legion made a fanatical last-ditch stand during the fall of Berlin to the Red Army – hardly the act of those uncommitted to the Nazi ideal.

When Westward Ho got under way, any thought of detailed screening of the refugees to weed out war criminals went to the wall because of the sheer numbers involved – 11,500 in the first two months. There was a further problem in that the CROWCASS, the Central Registry of War Criminals and Security Suspects, was woefully inadequate for all but German and Austrian suspects. Very few east Europeans were listed. In the case of the Balts, MI6 were pushing at an open door as far as the Foreign Office was concerned. Britain was not the only country with a labour shortage. Wilkinson was particularly concerned that other countries, particularly France, 'will have skimmed the cream of displaced persons, particularly the Balts'.

This 'creaming', overtly to supply labour to industry and covertly to identify intelligence assets, was disguising a huge humanitarian problem. It was not only European nations who were looking in the refugee camps for recruits. Canada and Australia were making requests to the Foreign Office, 'to take as many refugees as possible in family units as present financial and shipping facilities permit'. One memo reports that 'we are already being asked (e.g. by South Africa and Iceland) for permission to recruit German labour . . . it is obviously desirable, in view of the continuing influx from the Soviet Zone, that considerable numbers of Germans should emigrate from the Western Zone.' The problem was that everybody had the same criteria: youth, fitness for work, stable families; no Jews, no Poles need apply.

In January 1949 a conference of forty-nine voluntary refugee agencies from eleven countries met in Berne to discuss the problem. Delegates agreed that the 'discrimination exercised by governments in the selection of refugees against nationalities, religions, and dependants incapable of self support' was failing to solve the refugee problem. Wilkinson's scathing comment was that the voluntary sector would 'do something constructive' if it solved what he described as 'basic problems such as the disposal of hard-core unaccompanied children'.

Screening for war criminals was all but abandoned by 1949, certainly amongst the groups which were of interest to MI6. Writing in the *Scotsman* in March of that year, John Finlay Stewart claimed: 'There must be at least many hundreds of thousands in occupied Germany under the control of IRO [International Refugee Organisation], the fit successor of the scandalous UNRRA. It is again engaged in screening operations, and in many cases the screening officer is obviously a Communist or fellow traveller. One, recently screening a Latvian camp, stated that it was a shame Latvians were not sentenced to twenty-five years' penal servitude, or, rather, repatriated, as the Russians would welcome them. No doubt they would and send them to augment the millions in their slave camps . . . The screening ejects all those who fought for their own Baltic lands against the Russians.'

Wilkinson at the Foreign Office was outraged and phoned his plant at the British League, Frances Blackett. 'She agreed,' Wilkinson wrote, 'that this was far from accurate but expressed considerable concern at the news that screening was still going on. I do not think we shall hear any more of this for the time being, but if the IRO stick to their present line we can expect trouble.'

The former MI6 officer Anthony Cavendish made no bones about MI6 using former SS men in their Baltic operations. He told Tom Bower in an interview in 1989 that 'if somebody was needed to do the job and if he had committed war crimes, I would use him to do the job, ones I felt essential'. Stewart wrote quite openly about wanting to 'train all these refugees, harden them to be centres of resistance in their own countries to the terror that now stalks in Europe'.

The guerrilla war being waged in the Baltic states was real enough. In Lithuania the Forest Brotherhood fought pitched battles with Soviet troops. In one battle in 1946 more than 200 Red Army soldiers were killed. The Lithuanians knew the ground, and the thick woodlands were a deathtrap for occupying forces. More often than not, Soviet incursions resulted in the odd death from a sniper's bullet, the odd sentry with a slit throat. Some of the Brotherhood had fought the Germans, but now it was the other old enemy who had returned and they welcomed back into their ranks members of the SS and the police battalions who had slipped into the forests at the end of the war rather than face trial and execution at the hands of the Soviets. To the Kremlin-controlled press they were an 'underground movement of bandit gangs who are enemies of the people'.

Soviet response bore all the hallmarks of Stalin at his most brutal. In Latvia and Estonia farmers were sent to the gulags for failing to meet state quotas at harvest time. Lithuanian agriculture was ruthlessly collectivised. Again, it is the small tragedies that catch the eye. A US agent reported in 1946 on the case of an old Lithuanian woman whose assigned quota was two and a half tonnes of grain. Her four arable acres yielded only 300 kilograms. When the militia came to arrest the woman for failing to meet the requirements of the Soviets, her daughter offered to serve as a substitute for her mother. The agent reported to Washington that she was taken to Riga prison and 'held for seven weeks without trial, during which time she declined an offer to free her if she would cohabit with an official of the militia. She was finally tried by a people's court and sentenced to two years' imprisonment and five of exile in Siberia on a charge of Kulakism.' Meanwhile, Soviet officers and local party officials removed all the livestock and fixtures from the farm.

Beria, the head of the secret police, was ordered to 'finish off the Baltic outlaws'. In the event, 500,000 Lithuanians, 450,000 Latvians and 200,000 Estonians were killed. Ethnic cleansing was carried out, replacing native Balts with Russians. Stalin ordered the deportation of 600,000 from the region to the labour camps of Siberia; only a third survived. To MI6 planners the Baltic states were a prime area for their policy of fomenting unrest within the USSR.

In 1948 an intact platoon of the Lithuanian Police Battalion under the command of Anton Gecas was brought to Britain from that mysterious haven for Nazi collaborators, northern Italy. He settled near Edinburgh, working as a mining engineer, and, as an MI6 informant, provided intelligence for the Baltic operations. In 1992 a Scottish Television programme exposing his role in the Holocaust was blocked by Gecas. At the subsequent libel trial Lord Milligan pronounced himself 'entirely satisfied' that Gecas had participated in the mass murder of thousands of men, women and children during the extermination of Lithuania's Jewish population. The British state continued the policy of obstructing Soviet attempts to extradite him, hardly surprising given the MI6 beans he could spill.

The Baltic network was a spectacular failure. Agents were trained in the gentler arts of espionage – radio operation and tradecraft – at a rented house in Chelsea known as 'School'. The more vigorous skills of a spy – outdoor survival, sabotage and silent killing – were acquired at the Commando training ground near Fort William in Inverness-shire. Agents were given false identities and learned their legends. They were issued with so-called L-tablets (cyanide pills). In 1949, with the help of Naval Intelligence, MI6 acquired a boat operating under the guise of a fishery protection vessel sailing out of Hamburg. The US agreed to participate and provided some much-needed cash. Operation Jungle was born.

In early May 1949 the false fishery protection vessel slipped out of Hamburg with five agents on board. At dead of night they made a perfect landing at Palanga Beach in Lithuania. The problem was that one of the party was a double agent, the Latvian Vidvuks Sveics. As they made for the cover of the forest, Sveics separated himself from the party and alerted the local security police. Two of the agents were killed in the consequent shoot-out. Of the two who escaped, one, Kazimieras Piplys, was later shot during a battle in a Lithuanian bunker. The second mission was as much farce as tragedy. The team landed successfully and were taken to the home of Father Valdis Amols. Amols, however, was part of a Soviet deception ploy, and the guerrilla group they joined didn't actually exist. The Americans fared no better. One of their teams literally parachuted into a Soviet trap.

Harry Carr, the head of MI6's Northern Division, was forced to make two trips to Washington, in a 'desperate bid to stop the rot'. The CIA were, rightly, convinced that the entire Baltic enterprise leaked like a sieve and was riddled with double agents. But even this assessment was short of the full extent of the penetration which was literally staring them in the face. The man taking notes as MI6 liaison officer was none other than the traitor and masterspy, Kim Philby. He later recalled that both MI6 and the CIA 'had their Baltic puppets, whose rival ambitions were usually quite irreconcilable. It was with some relish I watched the struggling factions repeatedly fight themselves to a standstill.' Carr vigorously denied that the network was compromised and ended the second Washington meeting by boasting that he would step up operations. Philby recorded that 'the meeting ended disastrously, with both Carr and his opposite number in the CIA accusing each other, quite justifiably, of wholesale lying at the conference table'.

Carr did not lie about continuing with Baltic operations and they went on as they had started: a series of unmitigated disasters. One agent, Zigmas Kudirka, recruited through the Westward Ho trawl, was dropped into yet another Soviet trap with a companion known as Edmundes, and spent three years of nocturnal existence hiding in a farmhouse attic. He eventually found a safe house. According to Nigel West in *Secret War*, when Kudirka finally managed to radio his handler in London for help, the reply he received was: 'Chin up. It's not so bad.' It was worse. He was arrested and sentenced to fifteen years. He discovered that Edmundes was, in fact, a Russian plant, and had his sentence reduced to two years after successfully arguing that he had effectively been working, albeit in complete ignorance, under Soviet control.

Ineffective as Western intelligence was in the Baltic, the guerrilla war continued until 1952. It is estimated that some 80,000 Soviet personnel were killed between 1945 and the end of armed resistance in the forests of Lithuania, Estonia and Latvia. In the Ukraine a guerrilla war of even greater ferocity and cost to the Russians was fought during the same period. It too was marked by botched Western espionage operations and consequent recrimination between Intelligence chiefs in Washington and London. In the words of Kim Philby, 'disagreements over the Ukraine were even longer drawn out and just as stultifying'.

Chapter Seven

Down on the Farm with the SS

John Finlay Stewart had more than a professional interest in the Ukraine. To one Foreign Office official he 'has swallowed the Ukrainian Nationalist line whole'. He could explode into racist ranting when considering Soviet rule in the region: 'Unable to crush the UPA, the Ukrainian Insurgent Army, he [Stalin] sent into the country battalions of Far Eastern semi-savages putrid with Siberian syphilis and handed over to them the Ukrainian women and girls and mere children.' In his days as an agent in the Soviet border lands he had met Stefan Bandera, the leader of that insurgent army, whose unit had behaved with such brutality at Lviv under the Nazi banner. To Stewart, Bandera was 'the personification of the Ukrainian resistance'. In the summer of 1946, his former right-hand man and close friend of Stewart, Yaroslav Stetzko, brought Bohdan Panchuk to the Edinburgh office of the Scottish League for European Freedom. At the time there were few Ukrainians in Scotland, but by October 1948 the Foreign Office estimated there were some 4,000 in 50 hostels, most of them in the Edinburgh area.

Panchuk was a Canadian Ukrainian who had served with some distinction in the RAF. He chaired the Ukrainian Relief Committee, and in this capacity was in touch with A.W.H.

Wilkinson of the Foreign Office Refugee Department. Indeed, the two men became close friends and frequent luncheon companions, so much so that the mandarin was known to Panchuk as Wilkie. One item dominated the agenda at this first meeting with Stewart: the launch of a propaganda campaign to secure the release of the Ukrainian SS Division being held in a POW camp at Riccione in northern Italy.

Quite how they got there at the end of the war is shrouded in mystery; how they managed to avoid being handed over to the Red Army as war criminals is bathed in deceit. The officer who had been sent to report on the division in 1945 was a Major Denis Hills. As a student at Oxford, Hills had been a fascist. Age had mellowed him into a hard right conservative of the authoritarian rather than Manchester liberal variety. He dismissed accusations of war crimes as Soviet propaganda and was impressed by the fervour of the unit's nationalist sentiment.

There were also motives of high military policy at work. There were fears of a Yugoslav attack aimed at seizing the port of Trieste, and of a Communist takeover in Italy. In a mirror image of Churchill ordering Montgomery to keep Wehrmacht weapons to hand for Operation Unthinkable, Britain was keeping an SS division to hand in case of border incursions or a coup in Italy. Panchuk even suggested that they could be formed into a British Foreign Legion, or simply incorporated into the army. On 29 March 1946 the Foreign Minister, Ernest Bevin, met UNRRA officials and they agreed to protect the division. The legal basis devised for this was that Galicia was an area of the Ukraine under Polish rule in 1939; hence their Soviet citizenship was in doubt.

Stewart busied himself producing a barrage of pamphlets

and letters to newspapers giving a highly creative account of events in the Ukraine during the war, and eulogising the role of Stefan Bandera and Yaroslav Stetzko. 'The Ukrainians, solidly organised,' according to one of his propaganda sheets, 'launched the fight against the Germans and Bolsheviks simultaneously.' Richard Stokes was brought on board to champion the division's cause on the floor of the House of Commons. Several pieces of important disinformation were disseminated, one of the most significant being that the unit had been formed in 1944, 'to be used only and exclusively on the Eastern Front against the Communists'.

The Westward Ho scheme proved to be the solution to the problem of getting the Ukrainians into the UK. With a general election in Italy bringing a centre-right coalition, the threat of a Communist takeover had receded and the presence of more than 8,000 SS in a camp near a small Italian town was becoming something of an embarrassment. Wilkinson, no doubt prompted by his friend Panchuk, was quick off the mark: 'If a mission were to be sent to Italy to recruit labour for this country, it would not only help solve a serious problem but would also show the Italians that we are doing our best to relieve them of a serious burden on their economy.' The mission went ahead, and in the event the task of examining the men fell to Brigadier Fitzroy Maclean and the Special Refugee Screening Unit.

Maclean found a security shambles. There was no list of camp inmates and one had to be drawn up using information from the Ukrainians themselves. There were no identity documents, so the men could in effect conceal anything that might prove to be somewhat difficult. In spite of that, those who were interviewed admitted they had volunteered and had not been conscripted. There were few camp guards, and it was more or less run by an 'extreme' Ukrainian nationalist leader. Maclean and his team were so overstretched that by the end of the operation it had only been possible to screen 200 men.

He reported that 'we only have their word for it' that they had committed no war crimes. In a 1989 television interview Maclean described the affair as a 'hopeless proposition' and admitted that there 'was every probability that there were war criminals amongst them'. He also confirmed that 'no further action was taken to check their wartime activities'.

Two extremely sanitised versions of the history of the division were circulating in Whitehall. One was a long memorandum which had been drawn up for the Ukrainian Liberation Committee by its former commander, Pavlo Shandruk. Shandruk had been a leading conspirator in putting the Promethean League together again in 1945 and resuming its pre-war relationship with MI6. The other, by Panchuk, had been drawn up with the help of A. Paliy, the head of the division's Military Council.

They basically carried the same messages about the date of its formation and its nature as a unit solely for use against the Russians on the Eastern Front. As with all good disinformation, there are nuggets of truth to act as the smokescreen for lies. It was perfectly true that the original Ukrainian Division grew out of Bandera's OUN guerillas. It was a lie that that they were, in some convoluted way, not SS. Panchuk was particularly creative in his version: 'In accordance with the general policy for all non-German foreign units the unit was termed "Waffen SS". This should not, however, be mistaken for the actual German SS.' This was nonsense. It was true that they were decimated at the Battle of Brody, and faced the full brutality of the Soviets. 'Many were destroyed in action,' Panchuk wrote. 'Many were captured by the Russians and immediately destroyed and massacred . . . many committed suicide and a very large number went underground to join the Ukrainian partisan units in the Carpathian mountains.' All of this was true, although he failed to point out that the partisan units would be fighting the Soviets, not the Nazis. He then claimed that 'upon their return to Neuhammer, they were all placed in concentration camps as traitors'. A lie. The commander of this original division, SS-Brigadeführer der Waffen SS Fritz Freitag, won the Iron Cross following the battle and issued his order for the day: 'We all vow to the Führer that in our new undertakings it is our intention to fight through together until victorious over the Bolshevik hordes and their Jewish plutocrat allies.'

The final claim was the coup de grâce of deceit: that the men in Italy were a 'Second Division' formed by the transfer of Ukrainians from other Wehrmacht units, or gleaned from labour camps, and that 'every means and method was used to compel every Ukrainian physically fit to join the unit'. All of this was deceit. What happened in March 1944 was not the creation of a new 'Second Division'; recruits joined the re-grouped remnants of the original 14,000 Waffen SS men who had taken such a pounding at Brody.

This was the doctored version of history given to Fitzroy Maclean when he tried to screen the men in Italy. It was also the version given to the hapless Minister of State for the Foreign Office, Hector McNeil. He was not regarded fondly by MI6. At the time of the split between Tito and Stalin he dined with the *New York Times* correspondent, Cyrus Sulzberger, and 'sneered at British and American Intelligence services', for knowing nothing of the row between the two Communist leaders. In June 1947 the Soviet Union protested at the removal to the UK of the Ukrainian Division, which they claimed, correctly, contained war criminals. McNeil lied, and told the Russians that this was an ordinary Wehrmacht unit that had been 'exhaustively screened'.

He misled the House, again describing them as 'ex-Wehrmacht' personnel who had been screened 'by a Soviet mission in August 1945, and a further cross-section was screened by the Refugee Screening Commission in February of this year'. He was then challenged by Barnett Janner, a Labour MP who was a leader of the Jewish community, who asked if his right honourable friend was 'aware that members of this division were exceptionally brutal', and that 'they had murdered hundreds of thousands of people in cold blood'. At this point Richard Stokes intervened, making his well-trodden speech about how the oppressed Ukrainian people loathed Russian and German equally and were merely fighting for the God-given right to have a homeland. McNeil's reply to Janner, when it finally came after the Stokesian rant, was that 'we have taken most extensive precautions' to ensure war criminals were weeded out and that he was 'in no doubt that there will be further screening processes associated with these men'.

If that was the intention it was never carried out. The policy was reiterated in a memo from the Foreign Office to the War Office, who would have to receive the men in two transit camps and wanted no long delays in getting them off their hands: 'They are to be scattered and used for labour and adequately screened at leisure afterwards'. When the IRO took over from UNRRA there was an increase in screening, but, as we have seen in the case of the Latvian Legion, this was something the Foreign Office wanted stopped. John Finlay Stewart waded in for the Latvians, and Panchuk put pen to paper in the Ukrainian cause: 'In spite of many assurances that were given that screenings had been completed and done with, a new screening is now being adopted . . . people have been over screened, under and super screened.' Clearly Foreign Office policy differed from the policy stated on the floor of the House of Commons or defined to other departments in memos.

The men were indeed scattered to refugee camps around the country prior to 'civilianisation'. Every effort was made to keep the true nature of this influx of refugees a secret from the public. In February 1948 a meeting of the Union of Ukrainians in London gleefully anticipated 'a large increase of membership in the near future when the men of the SS Galizien Division become free workmen'. Fortunately for the Foreign Office, the media did not pick up this all too public declaration of what had been going on. Officials decided that 'Panchuk should be warned against allowing expression of statements which may give the impression that SS men are being allowed to settle down in the United Kingdom.' Wilkinson wrote to his Ukrainian friend telling him that public statements on the division were 'most undesirable', and that he 'would be grateful if this subject could be treated with discretion'. Panchuk agreed with this entirely, 'so as not to leave an undesirable impression on public opinion'.

Beyond the confines of the Foreign Office, the War Office and the Cabinet Office, there was no consultation with other government departments. According to the Ministry of Labour official, J. Tannahill, 'the Home Office and the Ministry of Labour were presented with a fait accompli'.

In March 1948 Panchuk compiled a memorandum for the Foreign Office detailing what happened to the division once they had landed in the UK, a document not released into the public domain until 2003. There were 8,361 of them and they were placed in 24 camps and hostels around the United Kingdom. The largest single contingent, 965, was housed at a former POW camp at Haddington in East Lothian. The camps were sited in rural areas and, aside from Haddington, those containing 400 or more were at Allington, Tattershall Thorpe, Victoria (in Cornwall), Botesdale, Fakenham, Wellingore, Carburton and Barony Camp. The men were largely used, under the Westward Ho scheme, as farm workers.

Panchuk described the majority of the men as 'of peasant stock with agricultural training', and stated that 'all of them are potential settlers and colonists', politically anti-Communist and 'opposed to all forms of autocratic government'. According to Panchuck, this SS unit was Western-minded and had 'developed in the democratic way of life as understood in the West'. something he attributed to the 'large number of relatives and friends in Canada, the United States and countries in South America', and he waxed lyrical on their soldierly virtues. He described them as disciplined, honourable and loyal men who had chosen to follow a 'true, honest and legal path'.

This was no collection of ignorant peasants. Not all of the men were agricultural workers, and even of those who were only 816 were classified as unskilled labour. More than 2,000 were 'technicians and skilled workers', including doctors, teachers, chemists and engineers, and there was a rich cultural life in the camps. They had set up thirteen choirs, eleven orchestras, six drama groups and seven wood-carving clubs.

There were even what Panchuk described as five 'dance ballets'. The mind boggles at the SS in tights.

In the memorandum Panchuk listed the numbers who were ill or unfit for work. He reported that 4,262 were employed in labour outside the camps, 1,434 were employed in camp administration and, intriguingly, that he had, 'no information concerning 965 members of the unit'.

The Haddington camp, described in 1948 as Amisfield Park EVW Hostel, had housed German prisoners during the war. There is no evidence that these were anything other than ordinary Wehrmacht soldiers, and indeed some stayed on after the war and became valued members of the local community. To describe it as a 'hostel' would seem to be somewhat euphemistic; one resident of the town at the time remembered it as 'a collection of Nissen huts'.

In October 1948 Panchuk presided over a conference of Ukrainian camp leaders in Scotland, held at Amisfield Park. There were clearly tensions between the Ukrainians and the Poles, who were providing the bulk of the voluntary labour in Scotland, tensions which more often than not ended in a brawl. This was clearly not in the interests of at least one of the groups represented, the Amisfield Park hosts, who sought as low and benign a profile as possible. Panchuk's minute of the conference recorded that difficulties were exacerbated if 'the nationalities superimposed one upon another happen to be from national groups which, rightly or wrongly, harbour historic and traditional enmity. A number of cases were cited, particularly in connection with Poles and Ukrainians.' He told the conference that 'We in particular must be broad minded, understanding and tolerant.' He did, however, note that: 'For the greater part, cordial and friendly relations existed between the Baltic peoples and the Ukrainians.'

The proposed fate of those unfit for work provides an insight into how ruthless government policy was in the selection of people under the Westward Ho scheme. In late 1948 the Ukrainians were medically examined and 5,000 were approved as suitable and given a status equivalent to other European Voluntary Workers. The remainder, for various reasons, were deemed unfit and were to be deported to Germany, effectively dumping them in the still chaotic ruins of the Reich. According to Tannahill, the 'rest of the story affords an interesting example of the tempering of administrative action by well mobilised public opinion. A leading part was played by Mr Panchuck, President of the Association of Ukrainians in Great Britain.'

Orchestrated by Panchuck and the Scottish League for European Freedom, a campaign was launched bombarding government ministers, members of parliament and the press with letters, and the usual suspects in the Commons were mobilised to ask a succession of awkward questions. It is testimony to the success of the policy of quietly scattering the division that nobody raised the issue of war crimes. They even had the sympathetic ear of that bastion of liberal opinion, the *Manchester Guardian*, which on 4 June 1948 carried the story of Patient no. 59, a young man who had lost his sight after falling off a government lorry: 'A month ago this boy was strong, healthy, and looking forward with joy of life to continuing, with his fellow workers, his work in Britain's battle for food. He has no friends in Germany, to which, as a result of a work accident he is to be deported – to what? It is submitted that this deportation is not in keeping with the traditional principles and practice of the British people or of His Majesty's Government.'

The men gained further public goodwill by setting up their own mutual aid fund, out of which they could support those classed as unfit. In December Panchuk called a half-day strike of all Ukrainian workers in Britain, and the Archbishop of Canterbury waded into the debate with a letter to the Home Secretary supporting their case. The government caved in and the only forcible repatriations were of thirty-nine men with 'bad records'. These 'bad records' had nothing to do with war crimes, but related to more mundane criminal activities such as theft, brawling and habitual drunkenness.

The site of the Haddington camp has now reverted to its original purpose as a golf course. At the beginning of the war it was used as an army transit camp, then later as a POW camp for German prisoners. As a camp for the Ukrainians it was a model of its kind: it had a choir, orchestra, drama company, and a full programme of sporting activities, though not, alas, a corps de ballet. It was well run and disciplined, with assembly and evening prayers to close each working day.

Religion was an important element in the nationalist movement. One of the concerns the men raised with Panchuk was that there was only one Ukrainian Greek Catholic Priest in the whole of Scotland, the Rev. W. Babj, and that there were no clergy of the Orthodox Church. Panchuk told them he hoped one of the SS Division's former padres, Iow Skalakalsky, could be delegated to Scotland to fulfil Orthodox needs. The Haddington inmates had their own teachers and education group, who aimed to promote a knowledge of their native culture and to improve English language skills. They complained to Panchuk of 'a great and crying need for literature and reading material in the Ukrainian language', but stressed that they did not want any materials emanating from the Soviet Union. The education group in East Lothian, unlike many other camps, managed to maintain English language courses with the help of local school teachers.

They marked the nationalist calendar. One photograph of the time shows the choir, in traditional garb, and the orchestra at a concert marking the three hundredth anniversary of Bodhan Khelinitsky entering Kiev following the rising of 1648 against Tsarist rule. In nationalist mythology this marked the founding of the Ukrainian Liberation Movement. At the heart of the camp was the outdoor chapel, its Ukrainian cross flanked by pictures of the nationalist leader, Colonel Eugen Konovolets and the guerrilla commander, Stefan Bandera. They created a symbolic mound, rather in the manner of a Scots cairn, to commemorate the fallen comrades of their SS Division.

As far as work was concerned, they roamed far and wide in the Scottish agricultural industry. They had a transport section of around thirty men based at the Dalkeith deer park, who 'transported members of camp to various agricultural establishments throughout Scotland'. They gained a reputation for hard work and, as most of them were skilled in the art and science of farming rather than merely being labourers, they gained a reputation for their professionalism. Beyond the environs of the camp their identities frequently confused the local inhabitants, and they were often described as 'Russians who fought with the Germans'. As John Finlay Stewart put it: 'Who are the Ukrainians? This was a very common question after the war when a large number of Ukrainians were brought to Britain as Prisoners of War who had been fighting against the Russians and had surrendered to the Western Allies. The answer to the question invariably was, "Oh they are a kind of Russian".'

One thing which may have aided the Ukrainians in developing their image and maintaining a low and benign profile was the simple fact that they were not Poles, and could be seen to have anti-Polish sentiments. Those sentiments would be perfectly in tune with the sentiments of many in the indigenous population. When immigrant labour was discussed at the TUC it was the Poles who were singled out as the group 'taking British jobs'. The British League for European Freedom launched a leaflet campaign to counter anti-Polish feeling around the UK, but scapegoating seems to have been particularly strong in Scotland. George Orwell, writing in *Tribune*, described overhearing two businessmen in a Scottish hotel as he was en route to Jura. The younger of the two accused the Poles of buying up 'all the houses', and of founding their own medical school and dominating the medical profession, while 'our lads' found it impossible to buy practices. The older made the bizarre claim that one of Europe's most pious peoples had, 'degraded morals and were responsible for much of the immorality nowadays'. Both agreed that the Poles should go back to their own country.

Stewart took a particular interest in the educational programme at the Haddington camp and published a series of books, 'Today's World', under the imprint of the Scottish League for European Freedom, which he distributed there. These were actually produced in Munich, now centre of the MI6- and CIA-funded Anti-Bolshevik Bloc of Nations, the ABN. Bandera himself, after linking up with remnants of the Slovak pro-Nazi Hlinka Guard for some last-ditch fighting against the Red Army, had fled west to find refuge in the British Zone of Germany. He moved to Munich and reformed his OUN organisation, but was forced to move to a remote Alpine house where he was protected by US Intelligence.

One of the demands made to Panchuk by the Haddington inmates was for a 'Ukrainian House' to be set up in Edinburgh. This became Stewart's main contact point after the unit were discharged into normal civilian life. His friend George Waters wrote of his charitable cover that: 'he set himself to do all he could to collect parcels and other necessaries, and took an active interest in the running of the Ukrainian House'. MI6 plans were gathering apace to send new Intelligence assets into the Ukraine.

In Munich in 1948 the ABN was hugely expanded under the presidency of Stetzko and took over Intermarium in an attempt, ultimately doomed, to bring together the traditionally factious Ukrainian national movements under a single con- trollable Banderite umbrella. They published the 'Chuprynka Plan', named after the self-styled 'General' Taras Chuprynka, who was now the leader of the Ukrainian Insurgence Army, the UPA, fighting the guerrilla war on the ground. The plan itself was a restatement of federal plans for the break-up of the USSR, but, the Foreign Office concluded, with the Ukraine 'the most powerful nation' within the federation.

This escalation of Intelligence activity around the Ukrain- ians was prompted by a growing sense in military circles that a Third World War was imminent. The gung-ho US Military Governor in Germany, General Lucius Clay, believed in March 1948 that it was six months away. The British Field Marshal, Bernard Mongomery, noted in his diary that 'he might well bring it on himself by shooting his way up the autobahn. He is a real he-man.'

Down on the Farm with the SS

The same year the CIA's Frank Wisner came to Germany as director of the Office of Policy Coordination, a grand-sounding title which meant he was responsible for covert operations, including paramilitary activities. At thirty-nine he was fat and balding. With a large gut hanging over a too-tight belt, he looked as if he could have played a part in a Hollywood film noir of the time as the doughnut-munching bad cop on the take. It was he who, at the end of the war, had convinced Allen Dulles, the station chief in Berlin, to switch from hunting Nazis to spying on the Soviets. In 1948 Wisner was candid about the fact that his mission was to set up a network of guerrillas to slow any possible advance when the expected attack came. 'Our policy,' he declared, 'is to support the cause of freedom wherever it is threatened.' To that idea, so beguiling to Western Intelligence, that the USSR could be destabilised by internal unrest, there was added the notion that the guerrilla movements could be used in fighting the Third World War.

The brutal guerrilla war in the Ukraine had already cost the Soviet Union and Poland dear, with an estimated 35,000 secret police and soldiers killed between 1945 and 1947. In 1945, in familiar style, Stalin began a process of ethnic cleansing, agricultural collectivisation, and rapid industrialisation using slave labour. He appointed Nikita Khrushchev, the future Soviet leader, to take charge of the region's post-war reconstruction. Faced with increasing attacks, Khrushchev and the local chief of the NKVD (the predecessor of the KGB), General Ryassny, launched an offensive using the Red Army, with its conventional tactics and weaponry of aircraft, tanks and artillery, attempting to draw the UPA into pitched battles where the Soviets could use their superior

141

firepower and technology to best advantage or, by sealing off areas, encircle the insurgents and annihilate them.

Although several battles were fought, the UPA increasingly used the unconventional methods of the guerrilla. They mined roads, railway tracks, bridges, and even river beds. The bulk of them withdrew into the forests in the foothills of the Carpathians, where the terrain gave the advantage to the guerrillas and turned the tank into a lumbering human cooker. Small units built underground bunkers and launched raids on local Communist Party headquarters, Red Army barracks and NKVD posts. The technique was first to isolate the target from the outside world by cutting the telephone wires before launching the attack. They ambushed military columns and blew up military trains.

They did not, however, solely rely on the tactics of terror. They found a psychological chink in Soviet armour – the use of ordinary Red Army soldiers – in this offensive. According to Oleh Martowych of the UPA, 'We developed an uncommonly strong political campaign which began to influence the troops. The freedom-loving, revolutionary slogans of the UPA found a lively echo among the Red Army soldiers who had just returned from the front in Germany.' It is just as likely they were simply squaddies who, having endured and survived four years in the cauldron of the war with the Nazis, had no great stomach for the brutish uncertainties of a guerrilla war, and were simply war-weary. Martowych claimed that Red Army units began to avoid engagements with the UPA, and, 'even aided us with information'.

How much of this is propaganda is a moot point; what is incontrovertible is that Moscow withdrew ordinary Red Army units and replaced them with battalions of security police, the

Down on the Farm with the SS

MVD-MGB troops, trained in anti-guerrilla warfare. They were selected from the far-eastern republics, Siberia and the Leningrad area, and were told they were going to fight the remnants of an SS division, collaborators and criminal elements who were hiding in the Carpathian Mountains. The leadership of the Ukrainian Catholic Church were, in Stalinist language, 'liquidated', the bishops either shot or sent to the gulags. Villages were torched and whole areas of forest bombed with incendiaries to deprive the guerrillas of cover.

As in most wars of this nature, however, atrocities were not confined to the one side. The UPA murdered or cut the limbs off peasants who co-operated with collectivisation. As with all terrorist actions, there were substantial deaths and injuries to innocent civilians caught up in bomb blasts aimed at Soviet officials. CIA-sponsored professional hit men carried out assassinations. Known as mechanics, they were usually Ukrainian but included 'some Scotsmen'. Fletcher Prouty, a US airforce officer who worked with the CIA on these missions, told Maris Cakars: 'I don't know how the Scotsmen got in there, but there they were.'

In the run-up to the expansion of the Anti-Bolshevik Bloc of Nations, the supporters of Bandera and his OUN launched a terror campaign in the displaced persons camps in mainland Europe. The OUN had its own secret police, Sluzhba Bezpeky (Ukrainian for Stay Behind), the SB. Throughout the camps, opponents of Bandera were rounded up, tortured and killed. Amongst those swept up in this reign of terror were people who knew too much about the pro-Nazi past of the Banderites and their role in the Holocaust. This all grew out of an American operation called Ohio, which they quietly allowed to be taken over by the SB. It was carried out under the personal direction of Bandera himself, and Yaroslav Stetzko.

As the Soviets began to have their brutal successes, the nationalists' propaganda became ever more lurid. It was from the UPA's Oleh Martowych that John Finlay Stewart got his line on syphilitic Siberians deliberately infecting the local population. Martowych described 'units from Siberia which consisted of men ill with Siberian syphilis. They were ordered to spread this kind of syphilis among the population, and for this purpose they were allowed to rape even the minor girls to infect them with this frightful disease.' Martowych also claimed that the Soviets sold serums of typhus and other diseases disguised as medicines on the black market. Brutal as the Soviets were, all this smacks too much of crude propaganda to be true, coming as it does from an inherently racist nationalist group. The Ukraine endured a terrible fam- ine in 1946, with consequent outbreaks of epidemics, includ- ing typhus – the famine was at least in part due to the continuing guerrilla war.

The truth is that by 1948 this war was all but lost by the Ukrainians insofar as large scale operations were concerned. Soviet successes were hidden from their MI6 backers, Intelli- gence reports were fabricated, as were photographs of military actions, which were actually staged in the Bavarian Forest. In early 1947 a UPA unit ambushed and killed the Polish Foreign Minister, General Karol Swierczewski. This led to a joint operation with the USSR, Poland and Czechoslovakia joining forces to launch 'Vistula', a ruthless counter-insurgency cam- paign which included mass deportations of peasants deemed sympathetic to the nationalist cause, and the recruitment of spies within rural communities. The behaviour of the nationalists' own security service, the SB, in trying to root out these spies brought a slump in support amongst the peasants. As the effectiveness of Operation Vistula took hold, several thousand of the guerrillas fought their way across 1,500 of rough terrain to the American Zones of Austria and Germany in what Ukrainian nationalist mythology came to call 'the Great Raid'.

So, just as the UPA was being reduced to a terrorist nuisance rather than a threat to the security of the USSR, MI6 were embarking on an expansion of their support for Ukrainian insurgency. Intelligence from the region had all but vanished. The CIA claimed to have received couriers in 1949, but the quality of the information suggested that they 'were tramps who had wandered into the wrong country'. The Foreign Office, however, were closer to the truth of what was going on than MI6. Their 1949 overview of 'Ukrainian Insurgency and Émigré Organisations' concluded that the time had passed for fomenting a rebellion in the region to destabilise the USSR, and that the groups were so weak that they might only prove of limited value in Intelligence gathering. Meantime, MI6 pressed on with its own policy in the face of near-zero Intelligence to back it up.

Sending agents into the Ukraine proved as disastrous as sending them into the Baltic. In overall charge was Harry Carr, with Colonel Harold 'Gibby' Gibson running the operation, codenamed Integral. Gibson was yet another old MI6 hand who had been born in Russia before the revolution. The first mission was to prove a template for them all. A three man team took off from a Turkish airfield in an unmarked RAF aircraft with a Czech aircrew. They flew through Soviet airspace, in dead of night, at only 200 feet to avoid radar detection. Within five miles of the drop zone near Kiev they rapidly climbed to 500 feet, the minimum safe limit for a parachute drop. As they dived back to 200 for the hazardous return flight the Czechs confirmed the agents had landed safely. The aircraft successfully returned to base. Nothing more was heard of the agents.

The CIA fared no better. In September they dropped a two-man party near Lviv and a little later four agents were parachuted into the Carpathians. Aircrew reported both parties had landed successfully. Nothing more was heard of the men until the Soviet Union formally complained to the UN about a US-backed incursion involving former Nazi collaborators. The agents were taken to the Lubyanka, tortured and shot. As was customary, their bodies were burned in the basement furnace.

Working under the cover of being First Secretary at the British embassy in Istanbul that summer was Kim Philby.

Chapter Eight

The Master Spy

The biggest single émigré insurgency betrayed by Kim Philby was Operation Valuable, a joint MI6 and CIA plan to overthrow the Albanian Communist government. Philby was the British representative on the Washington-based committee that planned the operation. The British provided Malta as the base for training hundreds of émigrés, with the US providing most of the finance and air support from their Libyan base. Albania had been chosen because it was felt to be the smallest and weakest of the Soviet satellites, and, unlike many of the other operations involving refugee groups, this one went ahead fully sanctioned by the British and US governments, with the State Department and the Foreign Office maintaining close supervision.

There was much wrangling over the leadership of the proposed revolution. The CIA had set up an émigré front, the Albanian National Committee, led by a somewhat self-effacing young lawyer called Hasan Dosti. He does not seem to have been exactly Byronic freedom-fighting material: Philby was told he had to be handled very carefully because he 'scared easily'. The British choice was a former tribal chieftain and local warlord called Abas Kupi. Kupi, a supporter of King Zog, had fled the Communist regime and set up, with MI6 help, the Albanian Freedom Movement with bases in Greece and Italy. According to Philby, Kupi was 'whiskered and habitually armed to the teeth – made to measure for British paternalism'. Philby's assessment of the two rivals was characteristically laconic: 'If Dosti was a young weakling, Abas Kupi was an old rascal.'

One of the old rascal's friends was Julian Amery. Amery had been dropped into Albania during the war as a Special Operations Executive agent, part of a group of operatives known as the Musketeers. Along with another of the Musketeers, Neil McLean, Amery was employed by MI6 in 1948 as an adviser to the service on the country. In Voigt's magazine, *The Nineteenth Century and After*, he also acted as the service's chief propagandist, setting out the case for MI6 to be involved in special operations in the old wartime style, setting the Communist world ablaze, as it were. He argued that it was time to launch 'insurrections or sabotage campaigns in the Balkans or Turkestan', and to 'build up a powerful resistance network behind the Iron Curtain' and in places threatened with Communist takeover. He set out ideas for local resistance to be backed up with professionally-trained saboteurs and agents and pleaded the MI6 case: 'It takes time to train the directing cadre of liaison officers and sabotage experts. It takes time to lay the foundations of local resistance organisations . . . It takes time to build up the apparatus of communications and supply.' It is perhaps a pity he did not take his own advice. This was written in March 1949, whilst Amery was involved in pressing ahead with Operation Valuable. The green light was finally given at a meeting in Bucks Club with the CIA's Frank Wisner, and in December 1949 the first group of Albanians was landed.

They were, for some unfathomable reason, given the code name of Pixies. They were, of course, instantly picked up, tortured and shot. Soviet Intelligence, meantime, used the captured radio equipment to signal back to base that all was well with the operation and that contact had been made with local opposition forces. This was the signal for the other Albanian insurgents to be landed by boat or parachuted in. All found Soviet and Albanian troops waiting for them, and around 300 of the émigrés were killed in the ensuing fire fights. One small group, charged with Intelligence gathering, either by accident or design on the part of the Soviets, did manage to fulfil their remit. They escaped through Greece but, according to Kim Philby, 'the information they brought was almost wholly negative'.

Undeterred by yet another failure, MI6 pressed ahead with their insurgency plans, in particular, their plans for the Ukraine. The key players in identifying assets for this region amongst the former Galizien SS were, of course, John Finlay Stewart and the Scottish League for European Freedom. In the heatwave of June 1950 Stewart gathered together representatives of twenty of the émigré movements, operating under the banner of the Anti-Bolshevik Bloc of Nations, for a conference in Edinburgh. What was arguably the largest single gathering of Nazis since the last Nuremberg rally met on 12 June at the city's Central Hall.

The speakers on the platform at the public session of this Convention of Delegates from the Resistance Movements in Europe and Asia were a typical cross-section of the political hue of the delegates as a whole. Stetzko, of course was there. Belorussia was represented by Stanislav Stankievich, former Intelligence Minister in the Nazi's puppet government in

Minsk, who, during September and October 1941, had sanctioned the massacre of over 37,000 'Jews, Communists and
undesirables' with a brutality which surprised even the seas-
oned Einsatzgruppen. Their speciality had been to rape young
girls before shooting them and to crack open the heads of
children before consigning them to the pits. He had also
organised the formation of the Belarus Legion, which had
fought not the Soviets but the British and Americans on the
Western Front. The Latvian Legion were represented by
Alfreds Berzins, who had organised the transports from Riga
to the death camps and who was awarded the Iron Cross for
his anti-partisan actions. The public session was opened by
General Colonel Ferenc Farkas, who had been an intelligence
officer in the pro-Nazi Arrow Cross Hungarian government
and had been responsible for the execution of thousands of the
regime's opponents.

Local public opinion was softened up lest anyone ask
difficult questions. Briefed by Stewart's unofficial public relations officer, the former *Scotsman* editor, George Waters, the
convention received sympathetic coverage from the Scottish
media. 'In Defence of Freedom, Religion and Culture' was the
Scotsman's headline. Waters also used his influence to get its
sister paper, the *Evening Despatch*, to run a series of articles
on eastern Europe and Communism in the run-up to the
convention. They commissioned David Perlman to write the
series of 'eye witness accounts on the extent of Sovietisation in
Poland and Czechoslovakia,' entitled 'This is the Enemy'. It
opened with 'Land of the Midnight Knock', a piece on the
secret police in Poland. 'This is,' Perlman wrote in dramatic
journalistic mode, 'the land of the midnight knock on the
door. I know because they knocked on my door and I

sweated.' The series examined Polish show trials, Czech purges and concluded that Communism was 'growing stronger on a policy of bread and terror'. The previous month the *Despatch* had run a somewhat lurid, almost McCarthy-like series – 'I spied for Moscow' – purporting to be by a former Soviet spy and detailing alleged links between Moscow and allied parties in the West.

MI6 political liaison was through Auberon Herbert, an old asset and Ukrainian specialist and Neil McLean, the former SOE comrade of Julian Amery with whom he had helped plan Operation Valuable. McLean was to become the Conservative MP for Inverness, winning a by-election in 1954. He became a kind of Richard Stokes for the 1950s and '60s, an MI6 representative within the governing party in the House of Commons. However, things did not go well. He was to last just ten years as the member for Inverness. McLean was an MP who did not tend his flock and was simply spending too much time on MI6 business, particularly in the Middle East.

In 1964 a quiet-spoken young schoolteacher, Russell Johnston, came in from the glens of Skye and stood against him as Liberal candidate. Johnston was always the gentleman and never attacked his opponent personally. However, some of his supporters were of a different cast: they dubbed McLean, 'the member for Oman', spreading the story that in ten years the MP had spoken for a total of six minutes on the floor of the House on matters concerning his constituency. McLean was trounced.

Problems with the drains in Inverness or the pot holes of Drumnadrochit were not exactly his style. He was the kind of person entranced by the conspiratorial; the factional world of émigré plotting was in his very life blood, driven, perhaps, by what John le Carré called 'the incurable drug of deceit itself'. He relished the atmosphere of the Anti-Bolshevik Bloc of Nations, the ABN. His biographer wrote of him that 'its very name was music to his ears'. He was an expert on the languages of the ethnic minorities within the Soviet Union and was able to converse with the leaders of the Ukrainian, Turkestani, Georgian and Azerbaijani delegations. He could even speak the obscure dialect of the Kalmucks, a tribe of the Cossack peoples.

For all his undoubted intelligence, McLean failed to learn two major lessons from Operation Valuable and to apply them to the continuing enthusiasm for fomenting revolution within the Soviet Bloc so evident at the Edinburgh convention. The failure to agree on the leadership of the Albanian adventure was a pointer to an endemic problem in almost all of the areas being targeted, tribal lands riven with ancient feuds, religious and ethnic conflict. In the unlikely event of Valuable having succeeded, the country would have been torn apart by competing war lords, tribal chiefs, ethnic cleansing and Islamic fundamentalism. It was a lesson learned by the Foreign Office Research Department, FORD, an organisation much despised by MI6 as being a bunch of academics out of touch with the real world. Just months after the Edinburgh convention FORD concluded that breaking up the Soviet Union along old ethnic lines would 'put the clock back four hundred years'.

The other unlearnt lesson was the propaganda of the émigrés themselves, which woefully exaggerated the strength of guerrilla movements on the ground. The small Intelligence-gathering group that survived to tell some of the tale of

The Master Spy

Operation Valuable did not find a country seething with revolt. As Philby put it, the 'infiltrators could achieve something only by penetrating the towns, which were firmly under Communist control. For bare survival they had to hide in the mountains.' There they found a world unchanged in a thousand years, a world of tribal chiefs who found the clandestine warfare being suggested to them dishonourable and unmanly. They also found the whole murky business of espionage untrustworthy and could not be convinced that they would receive overt Western support. The reality did not match the picture of a people ready and armed for rebellion painted by the émigré Albanian organisations.

At the convention, Stetzko claimed that if war broke out with the Soviet Union the Ukraine was 'in a position to set up an army of ten million soldiers'. The faked pictures of guerrilla units in the Carpathians were circulated, and Stetzko spoke of a 'new crusade in friendly collaboration with the resistance groups inside the USSR' which would 'alone be capable of saving the world from the Bolshevik menace'. Although it is doubtful if anyone actually believed Stetzko's figure of 10,000,000 soldiers, MI6 continued to believe that the Ukrainian Insurgency Army was still a major force.

The convention did, of course, have some considerable value as a propaganda tool. Frank Wisner, paymaster of many of the networks, believed that the émigré groups had 'tremendous value', not just for espionage and sabotage, but 'as propagandists and agents of influence'. It is astonishing to a modern journalist that this audacious gathering of so many war criminals produced not one sceptical piece, or even one sceptical question at a press conference chaired by Ferenc Farkas. 'We offer the western countries,' he told the

153

assembled hacks, 'our knowledge and experience of fighting against Bolshevism. We place at their disposal our love of freedom, anti-Communist feelings, and underground movements.' He was followed by that other war criminal Yaroslav Stetzko, who repeated his 'ten million soldiers' line and appealed to the West to 'gain the confidence of the oppressed peoples' who had been 'betrayed' in the past by treaties with the Soviet Union and, before that, by entente with Imperial Russia.

Stetzko was introduced as chairman of the ABN and former prime minister of the Ukraine. It occurred to no one to ask when he had been prime minister, a simple question, which, combined with some simple mathematics, would have revealed him for the Nazi collaborator he was. This, however, was both an age of deference and an age before ready access to vast quantities of raw news and information allowed one quickly to brief oneself on far-away countries of which one might know little. It is doubtful if such a presumptuous event could have got past today's press pack, for all its many ills. The only sceptical note came from the Poles, who had not been invited. They issued a press release which was not just sceptical, but realistic. Accusing the Ukrainians of not facing 'harsh reality', the Polish assessment was that 'today any active resistance against the Russians would be lunacy: it would bring only repression, massacres and mass deportations, without even the slightest hope of achieving the aim so much desired'. It was largely ignored by news desks.

The propaganda value of the convention was not primarily directed at domestic consumption. It was widely reported on the World Service of the BBC, Voice of America and the numerous CIA- and MI6-backed radio stations directed at the Soviet Bloc. Moscow produced counter-blasts describing the meeting as 'counter revolutionary' and the delegates as 'bandits, terrorists and fascists'. For a few days in June 1950 Edinburgh was at the dark epicentre of the Cold War propaganda battle.

The propaganda battle aimed at the UK had been stepped· up by the Soviets in 1948, the Foreign Office Russia Committee noting that 'the Soviet Government and their satellites, both in word and deed, have shown themselves to be increasingly hostile to Britain, as well as to the political and social ideals which this country shares with other Western democracies'. This was the year in which the military believed a war was imminent. War did not come but it may well have been a close-run thing. The Soviet Union blockaded Berlin for 320 days and the city was supplied from the air by the western powers. The climbdown by Stalin set the template for the Cold War in Europe, a war of espionage and propaganda.

Some of the former Ukrainian SS men identified by MI6 as assets in Edinburgh were sent to a secret language school located at a former RAF base at Crail in Fife. During the debate in the House of Commons on the War Crimes Bill in 1990 the MP Rupert Allason, who writes on Intelligence matters under the nom de plume Nigel West, told the House: 'The Ukrainians went to Crail, and I have evidence from people who served there and were taught Russian by people who openly boasted about the atrocities that they had committed against Jews in the Baltic countries during the war. Those boasts were known to British National Service men going into the Intelligence corps and they must have been known to the British Government in subsequent years.' Around 5,000 conscripts were trained at the school as signals monitors, interpreters and interrogators.

For the Ukrainians identified as potential agents on the ground, the prognosis did not look good. Even as they were being recruited, two further MI6 parties were dropped into the region, and vanished. Nor was all well with the Americans. Harry Carr visited Washington just before the Edinburgh convention to consult with his CIA counterparts. They raised doubts about Stefan Bandera's usefulness to the West and had reached the perfectly realistic conclusion that his guerrilla movement was a busted flush of no serious paramilitary value, which the failure of the British-sponsored parties seemed to vindicate. Taking notes at this meeting was, of course, Kim Philby.

Philby was arguably the most successful spy of the twentieth century, perhaps of all time. In nine years he rose through the ranks of MI6. He headed the Soviet section, moved on to be at the very centre of Cold War planning as the liaison officer with the CIA and FBI in Washington, and was being groomed to become head of the service. Churchill's description of the Soviet Union that Philby served so well fits the man himself: 'an enigma wrapped in a mystery'. His biographer, Philip Knightley, said that he had spent thirty years on the story, written hundreds of thousand of words on him, knew his family, friends and his widow, read every book written on Philby, and spent a week interviewing him and socialising with him, and yet 'whenever I am asked what he was like I have to reply that I'm not certain I know'.

He was a silver-spoon Communist of the 1930s. Born into a British colonial family, he trod the familiar path from public school to Cambridge University. At first he was attracted to the Labour Party, but was disillusioned by their defeat in 1931. In his view, 'a supposedly sophisticated electorate had been stampeded by the cynical propaganda of the day', something which 'threw serious doubt on the validity of the assumptions underlying parliamentary democracy as a whole'. As he described it in his autobiography, his journey towards Communism was an intellectual process, but it was more than that. There were two inspirational figures for him at Cambridge: the Marxist lecturer in economics, Maurice Dobb, and the flamboyant Communist David Haden Guest, a student fresh from a course at Göttingen University where he had taken part in street battles with Nazi stormtroopers. Yet Philby showed no affinity with the working class: two ex-coalminers he had befriended found him indifferent to the proletariat and to his own privileged background in equal measure.

Perhaps Graham Greene understood the process best from his Catholic perspective: 'Like many Catholics, who, in the reign of Elizabeth, worked for the victory of Spain, Philby had a chilling certainty in the correctness of his judgement, the logical fanaticism of a man who, having once found a faith, is not going to lose it because of the injustices and cruelty inflicted by erring human instruments.' For Philby, Communism was the one true religion, with its own holy writs, its icons and its terrible orthodoxies.

He was recruited into Soviet Intelligence by a remarkable agent, Arnold Deutsche, an Austrian Jew with a brilliant intellect and a taste for sexual as well as political liberation. During his posting in the UK he recruited at least twenty spies. Based in Hampstead, his cover was as an academic, taking a postgraduate degree in Psychology at London University. His recruiting strategy was to target young potential high-flyers from the better universities who displayed a left-wing bent.

Philby had returned from Vienna, where he had worked for the International Workers' Relief Organisation and tasted at first hand the violent politics of the streets. There he had been confirmed in his view that the only bastion against the Nazis was Communism. He also tasted the joys of sex in the snow with an Austrian Communist, Litzi Friedmann, whom he promptly married. On his return to the UK it was probably through a friend of his new wife, Edith Suschitsky, that Deutsche made contact with Philby. Philby had been thinking of joining the Communist Party, a move which would have made the career he was to have impossible. He was taken on a long circuitous taxi journey by 'an Austrian friend', to a meeting which took place, in the best traditions of the worst spy novels, on a bench in Regents Park.

Philby recalled to the Russian writer Genrikh Borovik that Deutsche told him that if he joined the party he would become one of many thousands of Communists. 'Let's say you distribute leaflets on the street,' Deutsche said, 'but anyone can do that, you don't need your education for that. You came down from Cambridge. You have a marvellous career ahead of you . . . you have to help us that way' – the old dictum of Tallerand: 'If you wish to destroy the state, become the state.'

It was through Philby that Deutsch recruited the other former Cambridge students – Anthony Blunt, Guy Burgess, John Cairncross and Donald MacLean – to form a spy ring that was to penetrate far into the British establishment, from

158

Intelligence, through the Diplomatic Service into the very corridors of Buckingham Palace. To their handlers at Moscow Centre they were 'The Five', later 'The Magnificent Five'.

Even were they to survive Philby's betrayal, the prospects for the new Ukrainian recruits to be parachuted in during 1951 grew bleaker by the day. In late 1950 the Soviet government launched an amnesty for members of the UPA and 8,000 handed in their weapons and gave up the armed struggle. Their supreme commander, General Taras Chuprynka, was killed at his headquarters in a village near Lviv. His parents were deported to the gulags and his wife and family 'disappeared', probably a euphemism for execution.

To make this bad job even worse, the Munich-based end of the UPA had been penetrated. Two Soviet agents, Pavel Sudoplatov and Ilarion Kamazuk, had managed to plant a Ukrainian double agent into the insurgency group that had fought its way out of the Ukraine in the so-called 'Great Raid'. When Bandera became worried at radio silence from his networks in the Carpathians he decided to send in the head of his security service (SB), Mynon Matwijejko. Matwijejko's party included the Soviet mole, and MI6 dropped the team into the Ukraine in the summer of 1950. Sudoplatov later recalled: 'We not only wanted to protect our own man, we wanted to take them alive.'

The party were kept under constant surveillance and grew increasingly desperate as they found that the resistance movement now largely existed only in the inflated Intelligence reports from the few disparate groups starving in half-ruined bunkers in the Carpathian Mountains. The collectivisation of farming had largely cut off guerrilla food supplies. Deportations had removed great swathes of supporters, penetration by the Soviet secret police created an atmosphere of mistrust amongst what depleted cells of resistance there were, and the cell at the very centre of Ukrainian nationalism, the Lviv network, was no longer functioning. The group gave themselves up. Matwijejko co-operated with his interrogators, and at a press conference staged by Soviet Intelligence, he denounced Bandera and called for Ukrainian peace and reconciliation.

The wrangling over support for Bandera continued between the CIA and MI6. 'Rather to my surprise,' Philby wrote later, 'the British stood firm and flatly refused to jettison Bandera.' The two organisations, 'with ill-concealed ill-temper on the American side', agreed to review the situation at the end of the summer. In order to prevent 'overlapping and duplication' the CIA and MI6 exchanged 'precise' information about the timing and coordinates of their operations through the British liaison officer, who was Philby.

He was therefore apprised of the 'names and arrival points of three groups of six men who were to be parachuted into the Ukraine'. He passed the Intelligence to Guy Burgess, the Cambridge spy who had successfully penetrated the Diplomatic Service. He was working at the British Embassy in Washington, and was en route to London for a spot of leave. When he arrived he gave the details to the member of the network who was the mole in MI5, Anthony Blunt, who passed it to his controller at the Soviet Embassy, Yuri Modin.

In late spring the three parties took off from Cyprus. They were dropped near Lviv. None was heard from again. Philby wrote, somewhat chillingly, 'I do not know what happened to the parties concerned. But I can make an informed guess.'

According to Philip Knightley, Philby showed no remorse for the unknown legions of agents he betrayed. He believed that this was a war, and that they were the enemy. He told Knightley that they 'were armed men intent on sabotage, murder and assassination. They were quite as ready as I was to contemplate bloodshed in the service of a political ideal. They knew the risks they were running. I was serving the interests of the Soviet Union and those interests required that these men were defeated . . . even if it caused their deaths I have no regrets.' He did admit that he sometimes felt badly about 'the necessity for this', as a 'decent soldier would feel badly about the necessity for killing the enemy in warfare'.

Not all of those he betrayed were killed, many were 'turned' by Soviet Intelligence, a process more often than not involving torture. In June 1988 the Soviets produced Feliks Rumniceks for the world's media. One of the Latvian agents who had been captured after a failed mission in 1945, his job had been to set up safe houses for Harry Carr's Baltic penetration missions and to provide information on Soviet army units. He was told the ultimate aim was to set up a network of agents to carry out sabotage and subversion. He communicated with Philby through an address in Stockholm, using the code Silenge. He went into Latvia through Finland and built up a network of ten agents. 'After about two years,' he said, 'we were all arrested. I was sentenced to twenty-five years hard labour . . . I didn't know until later that Philby was an agent for Soviet intelligence. I now believe it was Philby who betrayed me. My trouble was I was on the wrong side at the wrong time. I am no longer anti-Soviet.'

Philby always talked of the 'personal' and the 'political' as separate entities, though he was always clear that should conflict arise it would be the politics which would come first. Yet, on the personal level, like all good spies, he seems to have developed immense affability and charm. Years after Philby had defected to Moscow and confessed, Graham Greene fondly remembered long lunches at St Albans, pints in a pub behind St James's Street, a boss who would minimize or cover up small errors by one of his staff with a 'stammered witticism'. Greene viewed him as one ideologue views another, even if their ideologies were poles apart: 'How many a kindly Catholic must have endured the long bad days of the Inquisition with the hope of the future as a riding anchor? . . . If there was a Torquemada now, he would have known in his heart that one day there would be a John XXIII.'

I think in this case Greene missed the point – that Philby was not some innocent bystander but an instrument of the Inquisition. His comment is, however, an illuminating glimpse into the ideologue's mindset.

Although Philby himself always talked in terms of belief and of necessity, did he, like Neil McLean, enjoy the deceit itself? Murray Sayle, a *Sunday Times* journalist who met Philby in Moscow in 1967, certainly thought that 'the love of deceit and, by extension, of spying itself' kept him 'at his dead letter drops and secret inks all those lonely years'. His KGB controller, Yuri Modin, believed Philby never revealed his true self, and suspected he 'made a mockery of everyone, particularly ourselves'.

The Ukrainian fiasco continued through 1951 and into 1952, but with a new Soviet tactic. The Americans started using the Gehlen network and lost at least five missions and sixteen agents. We do not know how many British operations were mounted but the new tactic kept them coming to no good effect. The flow of apparent 'Intelligence' increased as agents radioed back; the twist was that this Intelligence was worse than useless as the agents had been turned and were operating under Soviet instructions.

John Finlay Stewart wrote in 1952 that 'many of the men are killed in action, but the gaps are instantly made up from among the people, and the whole nation is behind it [the UPA].' His lists of 'the fallen' give the impression of well organised guerrillas, reporting the deaths of chairmen of the Province Executives, sergeants in the Communication Service, commissioners for the Direction of the Foreign Units, or soldiers of the Security Service as if there was a large and disciplined underground army in the Ukraine.

The Foreign Office view, as early as February 1951, in reply to a letter from Stewart was that 'the strength of ethnic movements is declining, especially amongst the young, under Soviet influences'. FO officials also believed that the resistance movements, 'though still often active, are losing rather than gaining strength'. Disillusionment was setting in. Even Neil McLean was tiring of the inability of the Anti-Bolshevik Bloc of Nations to get their act together. Yet it was not MI6 who pulled the plug on Bandera, but rather Bandera who gradually distanced himself from British Intelligence.

All this highlights the curious extent to which MI6 was detached from official British foreign policy – that is, until you consider the fact that MI6 did not officially exist until 1992. On 6 May the then prime minister, John Major, stood up in the House of Commons and admitted what everybody knew anyway, that the UK had an external security service. Of course, parliamentary scrutiny was impossible if an agency of government did not officially exist. It is to the credit of the much-maligned Major government that he followed up the admission with the Intelligence Services Bill, which, for the first time, created a parliamentary committee, albeit one with limited powers and carefully chosen members, which can, at least in theory, shine some light into the dark corners of the secret world.

Although MI6 can trace a kind of lineage back to Elizabethan times, its modern manifestation grew out of pre-First World War hysteria and panic about German spies, fuelled by the populist ravings of a thriller writer, William Le Quex. In 1906 he published *The Invasion of 1910*, a lurid account of the Kaiser's 'hordes' landing in Britain after the country had been betrayed by spies and saboteurs, complete with Uhlans bayoneting babies in Hyde Park and English roses being ravaged by Hunnish brutes. He used a docu-drama technique and had hit on a winning formula. He churned out five such books a year, and in *Spies of the Kaiser* claimed to have a list of 5,000 German agents, including MPs, government officials and many of the good and the great of the age. Incredibly, he found support in Military Intelligence in the shape of Lt-Colonel James Edmonds. It is clear Edmonds did not believe the story, but he used Le Quex's ravings and the consequent public spy mania to get the government interested in beefing up British Intelligence.

The government set up a committee which laid the foundations of the modern Intelligence services. It mainly concerned itself with internal security and what would become MI5. When it came to consider actually spying on other countries there is a whiff of public school and gentlemen's club: spying was not quite the done thing but, as you had to do it with foreigners, you weren't going to admit to doing it. In a single paragraph of their report was born the detachment of MI6 from government: 'We are in a difficult position when dealing with foreign spies who may have information to sell, since their dealings have to be direct and not through intermediaries. They are therefore compelled to exercise precautions in order to prevent the government from becoming involved, which would be unnecessary if an intermediary who is not a government official was employed in negotiation with foreigners.'

MI6 didn't finally abandon its émigré operations until 1953, when it handed what remained over to the Americans. In the same year it withdrew its financial support for the Scottish League for European Freedom. John Finlay Stewart kept the organisation going, pouring out pamphlets, letters to newspapers and articles in the Anti-Bolshevik Bloc of Nations magazine. These became increasingly racist attacks on Russia and the Russians who, according to Stewart, 'had the instinct of conquest from the reign of Ivan the Cruel: they employed violence and artifice by turns, and succeeded with rare ability in augmenting their territory at the expense of their neighbours'.

He kept up his contacts with the Ukrainians who had settled in Scotland, and was a frequent and honoured guest at their club in Edinburgh. His 'most intimate and highly respected friend', the war criminal Yaroslav Stetzko, made frequent visits to the city, and they would mull over their glory days in the border forests of Russia in the 1930s. Sometimes the mask slipped in public: 'I am quite certain,' Stewart wrote in the ABN's journal of the Baltic and the Ukraine, 'that if Hitler had listened to his greatest generals and statesmen, and made all these countries sovereign independent states, the war would have had a different ending, in spite of American help.'

Plagued by increasing ill health, he died in August 1958. His old friend George Waters paid handsome tribute to him in an obituary in the *Scotsman* as a man who 'championed the cause of refugees'. The ABN's journal gave him a full page: 'Let the memory of John F. Stewart be honoured for ever in the annals of the arduous struggle.'

It is hard to grasp the place the SS Galizien division has in Ukrainian national mythology. After the fall of the Soviet Union the Ukraine erected a huge monument to the division. It is testimony to the enduring ethnic enmity that the Russian secret police blew this monument up. Closer to home, émigrés in Bradford persuaded the city's cathedral to erect a plaque in honour of those members of the Ukrainian SS who had been killed. As David Cesarani put it in *Justice Delayed*, 'Ukrainians in Britain combined perfectly respectable lives with unyielding allegiance to the ideals which led many of them into the Waffen SS in 1943–44. They behaved as if they had nothing to fear.' What can be said in their defence is that the peoples of the United Kingdom can take the moral high ground with perhaps too much ease. We were not the victims of Stalin, subjected to purges, a man-made famine, slave labour, extermination and deportation. Nor was the British mainland invaded by the Nazis. The one part of Britain where the Swastika did fly over the town hall was the Channel Islands, which proportionally produced just as many collaborators and overt pro-Nazis as any other part of occupied Europe. However, even allowing for all of that, the sheer brutality of the Ukrainian SS put them beyond the pale.

There is one final twist to this story, which takes moral and indeed legal judgement to one of the darkest places in the Nazi world: the experimental medical bloc of Auschwitz concentration camp.

Chapter Nine

The Road to Hell

In 1946 a dapper Polish army doctor, Vladislav Dering, arrived in Scotland. His own version of events at the time was that he had been a member of the Polish resistance who was arrested by the Gestapo in 1940 and sent to Auschwitz, where he worked in the camp hospital as a male nurse. He claimed he was later moved to a hospital in Silesia; when the Red Army arrived he managed to get false papers, made his way to Italy, and joined General Anders' Polish 2nd Corps.

It was a version of events that was conspicuous not for what it said of his life, but for what it left out. Joining the Polish 2nd Corps in the last two years of the war was a route many war criminals took in a bid to evade justice. At a Christmas party, in the company of some officers he considered like-minded, he drank too much. Always as well dressed as the exigencies of the times allowed, he boasted that 'my suit once belonged to a Dutch professor who went up the chimney'. He then claimed he had got his tobacco pouch from a prisoner and that it was made from the scrotum of a Jew.

At some point shortly after this he moved to London, an easier place to maintain a low profile and lose oneself than the small world of the Scottish Polish community. He had much to maintain a low profile about, for he appeared on CROW-

CASS, the Central Registry of War Criminals and Security Suspects. The charges against him were that he had worked for the Nazis in performing experimental sterilisation experiments on Jews in Auschwitz.

The sterilisation experiments were authorised in a memo from the 'Headquarters of the Führer' in July 1942: 'The Reichsführer SS [Himmler] confirmed to SS Brigadeführer Professor Clauberg that the Concentration Camp Auschwitz is at his disposal for his experiments on human beings and animals. A method is to be found causing sterilisation without the persons noticing it. All the persons participating in the experiments must be pledged to secrecy.'

Professor Clauberg was a doctor, Carl Clauberg, who was chief physician of the gynaecological clinic at a hospital at Königshütte in Upper Silesia. In May 1942 he had complained to Himmler of difficulties in procuring female concentration camp inmates for 'experiments in negative population policy'. He asked for facilities in Auschwitz to include 'occasional special billeting for five to ten women . . . corresponding to the conditions of sick rooms' and 'special X-ray apparatus'.

The issue of sterilising people without them being aware of it had arisen at the Wannsee Conference in January of that year, when the shape of the final solution was fashioned. Having decided that Jews should be exterminated there then ensued a long legalistic wrangle over the fate of people with Jewish ancestors and just how far back you had to go before a Jew of mixed blood became a German of mixed blood. The debate was a model of what happens when lawyers go wrong, for the vast majority of those attending the conference had a law degree. The upshot of this was that Germans of mixed blood should be sterilised and a means found to do this in secret.

In June 1943 Clauberg reported back to Himmler: 'The method I contrived to achieve the sterilization of the female organs without operation is as good as perfected.' It was on this programme, later expanded to include the sterilisation of male inmates, that Dr Dering was alleged to have performed experimental surgery without anaesthetic.

In January 1947 the Polish government asked for 'any assistance' in his arrest and extradition, and urged speed, 'as any delay may result in Dr Dering becoming aware of the charges against him and attempting to escape'. The Foreign Office were also told by the UN War Crimes Commission that he was wanted for questioning by both the Czech and French governments. He was interviewed by a Colonel Fortescue, who reported that Dering had been a straightforward general surgeon and had done a vast number of operations in the camp hospital under enormous pressure. 'No surgeon,' he concluded, 'could perform so many operations in a prison camp without making enemies and being accused of operating for operating's sake. I have heard such accusations in British hospitals.' Dering made much in this interview of a claim that he could not return to Poland because he had been born in Kiev and had taken part in 'anti-Bolshevik activities'.

MI5, however, began uncovering darker evidence. They sent a report to the Home and Foreign Offices on 24 January on an account of his activities from Dr Karl Sperber, a former Auschwitz inmate living in Prague. He described Dering as becoming 'so infected by the scientific zeal of his German colleagues that he soon became quite independent and started to perform his own operations'. Sperber claimed that the Auschwitz doctors showed 'great interest' in the survival of sexual urges in sterilised men and women, and would put the two sexes together: 'Through a spy hole in the door the zealous, objective scientists watched . . . They seemed satisfied with their observations.'

It was around this point that Kitty Atholl and the British League for European Freedom became involved, in what the duchess later described as 'the most difficult piece of work which had yet befallen the League'. They intervened on Dering's behalf and roused their powerful parliamentary lobby under the leadership of the indefatigable Richard Stokes, who set up a committee of MPs to lobby on the doctor's behalf. According to Kitty, at this early stage of the investigation they managed to get immediate action delayed through the offices of their secretary, Frances Blackett, the friend and informant of the Foreign Office mandarin, Wilkie Wilkinson.

The Dering affair was turning into a major diplomatic and propaganda problem for the Attlee government. Notes began to fly back and forth between the Polish embassy and the Foreign Office, whilst the Home Office dragged its feet. Radio Poland began to report the case: on 2 February BBC monitors recorded an item describing Dering as 'an assistant to German doctors who carried out experimental work. Every fourth day he selected people to be burned in the crematorium.'

The evidence against Dering grew apace. Dr Alina Brewda made a long statement to the UN War Crimes Commission which became central to this whole saga. She was a gynaecologist and had been a prisoner at Auschwitz from 1943 until 1945. She claimed in her deposition that Dering had told her he had performed 17,000 operations at the camp, of which 16,500 were experiments, performed on the orders of the SS. When Brewda doubted that so many operations could be carried out in so short a time, Dering boasted that within two hours he could perform sixty operations of testicle removal. In the case of female patients she 'saw with her own eyes' Dering perform operations on twelve girls, in two half-hour sessions, removing ovaries formerly X-rayed by Dr Horst Schumann, a Luftwaffe medical officer who had joined the sterilization research programme.

According to Brewda: 'Among these twelve women were two who had unhealed wounds after operations of removal of their right ovaries, performed six weeks earlier. One of the operated girls had a wound in the loins, festering after an X-ray treatment and reaching to the backbone, so that she could only with difficulty be placed on the operating table. The girl was fourteen. Dr Dering's operations were performed negligently, without assuring proper healing.' All of this without benefit of anaesthetic. One of the girls died within six hours, the other after three days. Brewda also claimed that Dering had taken part in the selections for the gas chambers and had been designated as Volksdeutsche, a Pole with sufficient German 'blood' to be admitted into the ranks of the master race, rewarded for his work by a posting to Clauberg's maternity clinic for SS families in Königshütte in Upper Silesia.

Dering was arrested and incarcerated in Brixton prison. To Kitty Atholl and the British League the accusations against him were the product of personal malice. The League's secretary, Frances Blackett, was charged with concentrating 'all her energies on collecting the evidence to clear Dr Dering'. To the duchess he was victim rather than perpetrator, the good doctor who had tended to the sick of the camp under appalling circumstances. 'Fellow ex-prisoners,' she wrote, 'and British friends who knew him were convinced of his innocence.' There is no evidence that the support for Dering was given with anything other than the best of intentions; Kitty Atholl sincerely believed in his innocence, and believed that he would not get a fair trial in Communist Poland. There is certainly no indication of the Security Services being involved in putting pressure on the duchess or the League to back Dering for some nefarious reason. Indeed MI5 were diligent in their collection of evidence, and it is probable, given that so much of it came from abroad, that they must have received help from their sister service responsible for external security, MI6.

There began an eighteen-month battle to prevent Dering's extradition, with the League's main weapon being its formidable parliamentary clout, under the command of champagne Socialism's prime anti Communist, Richard Stokes. One initial move proved less than helpful to Dering's case. The League tracked down former Auschwitz prisoners who had been saved from the gas chambers by the doctor. Colonel A. Jakobski testified that he 'knew of many cases, including that of saving my own person, when there seemed no way out, in which Dr Dering was successful in diminishing the number sentenced to death and getting others cancelled'. Konstonty Piekapski, another former inmate, said that 'Dering was able to prevent a number of prisoners from being put on the list by intervening with the German doctor; he also, at great risk to himself, took names off the list of people destined for the gas chamber.' Under interrogation, Dering was only too happy to confirm that 'he had saved people from extermination'.

All of this begged an enormous question – one raised by a Foreign Office official, F.F. Garner. Garner dismissed the argument that the case against the Auschwitz doctor was based on personal enmity and went on to argue that 'Dering admits that he played a part in selecting people for the gas chambers. This is murder. Whether or not he tried to get people off is beside the point. The fact is that he cooperated in sending people to the gas chamber and that is murder.'

Ian Roy of the aliens department at the Home Office was, however, less concerned with the morality of the issue, more with the administrative inconvenience and the embarrassment factor of having Dering on British soil. He wrote to the Foreign Office suggesting 'Emigration, perhaps to some South American country, may well prove to be the best solution.' Although the reply was that 'we should rather not have him here at all', Foreign Office opinion would seem, in general, to have been in favour of extradition. The Foreign Secretary, Ernest Bevin, was angered by attempts to let Dering off the hook he was: 'not impressed with this. I feel that all our concern seems to be to protect these monsters'.

Bevin certainly had a strong ally in the official handling the case for the Foreign Office, F.F. Garner. In March 1947 Stokes and the other BLEF supporters in the Commons raised the issue of Dering's continuing imprisonment without charges on the floor of the House. Garner had drawn up a note for his colleagues in the Home Office to brief the Home Secretary, J. Chuter Ede. Garner pointed out that the tail-end of the worst winter in living memory had delayed the delivery of the further evidence the Poles had promised, and told his counterpart in the aliens department, Carew Robinson:

I am sure it would be most undesirable to release Dering for the following reasons.
(a) He might use his liberty to work up demonstrations.

(b) He might escape and disappear, which would put us in a very awkward position with regard to the Polish Government.

(c) As he would almost certainly have to be re-arrested there would be criticism if we arrested him and then re-arrested him.

The next day, 4 March, Robinson lobbed a memo back, saying that: 'On the information before Mr Ede it does not appear that a prima facie case has been satisfactorily made out, and as Dr Dering has been detained for approximately six weeks, I am directed to enquire whether in Mr Bevin's view it is necessary to keep him in prison or whether Mr Bevin would agree that Dr Dering should be released subject to suitable restrictions.'

Mr Bevin most certainly did not agree. He raised the issue with the prime minister, Clement Attlee. Garner was able to reply to Robinson with full prime ministerial backing: 'I am directed by Mr Attlee to say for the information of Mr Secretary Ede that Mr Attlee much appreciates the action that has been taken in this connection.' The memo reiterated the objections to Dering being released, the expectation of more evidence from Poland, and pointed out that Dr Sperber, the Czech interviewed by MI5 in January, was expected in the UK at the end of the month. He ended the memo with a final flourish designed to put Robinson firmly in his place: 'In conclusion Mr Attlee would observe that Dr Dering has been charged with war crimes by three separate countries . . . it is felt that detention of two or three months is by no means unreasonable in the circumstances.' One gets the sense of a Whitehall skirmish won, and that Mr Garner, when he had hung up his bowler and umbrella that evening, would have had at least one sherry more than usual before dining.

It was, however, a skirmish and not outright victory. There was a problem with the evidence when it came. It was still circumstantial and there was no first-hand corroboration of the accusations made by Alina Brewda. Sperber proved a problematic witness. According to the investigating officer, he was sincere but prone to exaggeration. More importantly, 'his knowledge of Dering's alleged assistance to the Nazis is based almost entirely on hearsay, but he is intelligent and quick-witted and on the exceeding few matters within his own knowledge he would make an excellent witness'. Garner had to admit that there was 'little first-hand evidence here'.

According to Kitty Atholl's account in her autobiography, the Home Secretary 'took the unprecedented step of setting up a special judicial review'. Her economy with the truth at this point becomes a matter of omission rather than commission, for she makes no mention of the outcome of that review. Judicial reviews take time and it was not until April 1948 that Lord Jowitt, the Lord Chancellor, reported to Chuter Ede and advised him that there was indeed a prima facie case for extradition. The Poles had produced new and damning witnesses, including an actual survivor of Dering's surgery in the sterilisation experiments: 'the first-hand evidence we have been awaiting,' in Garner's words. The Home Secretary wrote to Bevin on the 19th, telling him: 'I have come to the conclusion that I must accept the Lord Chancellor's advice and am therefore giving instructions that the necessary action should be taken to give effect to this decision.' The Polish ambassador in London was informed that extradition would now take place.

Kitty Atholl's version was: 'Suddenly, in April, we learned that new accusations had been made against him, and were so damaging that the Home Office was on the verge of sending him back to what would have been certain death. The Polish government was bent on getting hold of him.' It did not occur to the duchess that the growing body of evidence against Dering might mean that he was, in fact, guilty of truly dreadful crimes against humanity. Her greatest strength was, perhaps, becoming her greatest weakness. Kitty Atholl stuck to her guns. Once she had decided something was right in principle she would not give ground – admirable when you are on the side of the angels, less so in the demon-haunted world of the final solution.

The British League for European Freedom sent a 'mass of testimony' in favour of Dering to the Home Office, and mounted a public campaign highlighting the summary nature of justice in totalitarian Poland. The committee of MPs formed to back Dering lobbied the Home Secretary, again highlighting the state of Polish justice. They told Ede that 'Polish justice is not justice by our standards and he would be condemned and executed out of hand'. One of their number, John Foster, acting as the doctor's legal representative, delivered a long memorandum outlining his case for releasing Dering; he also complained to the Home Secretary that he and his client had not had time to summarize and study the latest evidence. Ede felt that 'there was substance in this complaint', and in June informed the Polish government that deportation had been delayed.

Dering himself had now been in Brixton prison for more than fourteen months. Such was his state of mind that the authorities put him on suicide watch, believing that he might attempt to kill himself. In Foster's words, 'confinement under such terrible anguish is an extreme punishment'. He told Ede: 'It is quite clear that the Polish government's motive is political. Dr Dering was a member of the Polish underground and he was an anti-Communist. Mr Jozef Cyrankiewicz, the present prime minister of Poland, and Dr Brewda, a prominent Communist, both testify against Dr Dering. If the evidence of Mr Cyrankiewicz is examined, it will be seen to be nothing but hearsay.'

The BLEF and its supporters in the Commons spun the Dering story into one of a hapless victim languishing in Brixton under threat of being deported to a totalitarian regime to face summary justice and execution on flimsy or prefabricated evidence cobbled together for political revenge. 'The English sense of justice,' Foster wrote, 'must not allow a death sentence motivated by political revenge to be added to his long-drawn-out torture.'

The Foreign Office officials made one last bid to find a prop to support the argument for deportation. Its handling had passed from F.F. Garner to his boss, Sir Anthony Meyer, who asked the research department if they could find 'assuaging facts' on Polish justice to demonstrate that 'such trials in Poland are not necessarily unfair'. Geoffrey Shaw of the department found four cases which showed that 'a death sentence or an unfair trial are not always the rule . . . but it is very scant evidence to support the general thesis'. Sir Anthony went into Pontius Pilate mode: 'The Home Secretary is entirely responsible for the decision whether or not there is a prima facie case against Dr Dering such as would justify us in handing him over to what is recognised to be an unfair trial. He is, of course, influenced by political considerations. Our function in this affair is merely to act as a post office.'

In June Ian Roy of the Home Office aliens department asked the Foreign Office if there were any helpful precedents regarding the handing over of Yugoslavs for war crimes that could be applied in the Dering case. He was told that the public obligation was to hand over suspects against whom a prima facie case of 'active and wilful collaboration' has been established. 'This,' the Foreign Office memo made clear, 'is all that can be made public.' What was kept secret was that: 'We introduced special criteria in the case of Yugoslavs because it was clear that Yugoslav justice was a farce.'

Two thousand possible war criminals were protected by this hushed-up policy.

In August the Home Office found the flaw in the Polish case they were looking for. One inmate Dering had operated on had been found – a man who had had a testicle removed – but he failed to identify the doctor at an identity parade. Dering was released. To Kitty Atholl, 'It was an unspeakable relief to us all.' Sir Ernest Little, a friend of the duchess, secured Dering's re-admission to the British Medical Register.

It is hard now to understand that by 1948 there was a growing revulsion in Britain at the continuation of war-crime trials. There was no outcry in the British press about his release. *The Times* merely reported on a statement from the Polish embassy which said that in spite of Dering's release he would remain on the register of war criminals, and that the Warsaw government retained the right to take 'further appropriate action'.

What little sympathy there had been for the Jewish victims of the final solution had evaporated as the situation in Palestine deteriorated. Britain held the UN mandate in the region and Jewish demands for a homeland and the admission of

100,000 immigrants led to increasing violence. Three underground fighting groups, the Haganah, Irgun and Lehi, conducted a guerrilla war against the British army; in 1946 they
had blown up the army headquarters in the King David Hotel
with massive loss of life. In July 1947 the Irgun hanged two
British sergeants and the story received huge coverage in the
UK press, including a photograph of the bodies on the front
page of the *Daily Express*. There was widespread anti-Semitic
rioting in British cities. On the bank holiday weekend gangs of
youths in the south side of Glasgow smashed up Jewish shops
and homes, desecrated graves and attempted to vandalise the
synagogue.

The Nuremberg trials had little impact on domestic opinion.
As a historian of British attitudes to the issue, David Cesarani,
put it: 'All those involved were fed up with war and just
wanted to get on with the new exciting business of enjoying
the world at peace.' One journalist who covered the trials was
Peter Calvokoressi and he believed that the sheer numbers of
people murdered were so vast that they became meaningless –
impossible to grasp. He wrote in 1947 that, after the trials
ended, 'voices were heard in England urging a reprieve for the
condemned'. Cesarani noted another element: 'a feeling of
deep unease amongst the population and opinion leaders after
accounts of the horrors wrought at Hiroshima and Nagasaki'.

The trials of the ageing Field Marshals von Manstein, von
Rundstedt, von Brauchitsch and of Colonel-General Strauss,
in spite of the fact they had served the Third Reich to the end,
brought Winston Churchill to his feet in the Commons to call
for a 'stop to these denazification trials'. He had even donated
cash to the von Manstein defence fund. 'Revenge,' Churchill
told the House, 'is, of all satisfactions, the most costly and

long-drawn-out; retributive persecution is, of all policies, the most pernicious.' The UK abandoned war-crimes trials from 1 September 1948.

In this atmosphere it was relatively easy for Dering to slip into obscurity after his release. For eighteen months he worked in a London hospital before taking up a post in Somaliland, where his patients called him 'father'. He was, much later, to get his day in court, but in circumstances very different from the justice his victims sought in 1948.

Kitty Atholl, now in her mid-seventies, remained a formidable figure. On one occasion she made a trip to Aberdeen to recruit for her husband's old cavalry regiment. Communists had broken up a meeting there a few weeks earlier. As she began to speak, 'they made their presence felt'. The duchess commandeered one of the regiment's tanks, made her speech from the turret, and 'managed to silence them'. She made frequent visits to Paris, as British representative for an organisation called 'Nouvelles Equippes Internationales'. This was backed by Swiss banking interests and sought to promote Christian values, to fight Communism and work for European union. This was closely linked to the European Movement, a CIA-backed organisation which worked for the rapid unification of western Europe. Washington originally took an interest in the group to counter Soviet propaganda portraying the Marshall Plan, the US-funded reconstruction programme for the continent, as an American imperial Trojan horse. Kitty's friend, Elma Dangerfield, was a prominent British member of the European Movement, taking an active part in its work well into her eighties. Between 1949 and 1960 the CIA is estimated to have injected four million dollars into the organisation to drum up mass support for European integration, including the

Schumann Plan for coal, iron and steel, which led directly to the creation of the Common Market.

One of the architects of this idea was the State Department's George Kennan, a diplomat, historian and philosopher of Cold War tactics, whose influence extended into the 1980s. Unfortunately, the White House was not always listening. After the death of Stalin, Kennon argued that the US should exploit the subsequent liberalising trend and get into serious negotiations over the future of eastern Europe. In 1959 he argued for discussions to be opened with the USSR on reducing nuclear arsenals, and in the 1960s he was a leading critic of the Vietnam War. An early supporter of covert action in eastern Europe and the Soviet Union, by 1953 he had concluded that émigré groups had 'sold the US government a dangerous bill of goods'.

The British League for European Freedom went into decline at the same time as its Scottish sister, deprived of whatever funds it was receiving from Intelligence sources, probably American. It lasted, however, into the 1970s and became a creature of the ABN and Yaroslav Stetzko. Stetzko lived out his remaining days in the peace and quiet of a detached house in Wimbledon. Kitty Atholl attributed the decline of the League to the founding of Common Cause, a right-wing organisation whose purpose was to expose the 'subversive conspiracy' it believed was embodied in the Communist Party of Great Britain. It had a McCarthy-like agenda of rooting out individuals who might 'reasonably be expected to be engaged in activities detrimental to the welfare of the state'.

The final years of Kitty Atholl's life were probably not particularly happy ones. Her husband's disastrous business failures returned to plague her. In 1932 his financial incompetence had led to the estate being taken over by a company organised by the extended Atholl family. He was chairman, but effective control passed from his hands. Property and some of her jewellery had to be sold to pay debts. Post-war austerity left the estate on a still shaky financial footing, and Kitty's pied à terre at Eastwood was sold. She had one final 'happy summer holiday' there. 'It cost me a pang to leave it,' she wrote, 'with its many happy memories, but as I had been given rooms at Blair I could not complain.'

Kitty Atholl had many estimable qualities. She was an able member of parliament and had made a good job of being a government minister. Had she survived deselection she would have fitted into the wartime coalition, and into the Tory Party of the 1940s and '50s. Although right wing in her anti-Communism, her attitudes to social policy would have tuned in perfectly with the post-war consensus. From the perspective of Britain after Thatcher and the foundation of New Labour, it is easy to forget just how left of centre the Conservatism of Macmillan and Rab Butler was.

She was also a fundamentally decent human being, who willingly gave up her scholarship at music college to help a fellow student, and who worked hard for many charities, particularly Save the Children, which she had a hand in founding, and the Red Cross. It is easy to sneer at the good works of the laird's lady, but this lady faced bombs and bullets to rescue Basque children, nursed the wounded in the desert and forced through real progress in medical services in rural Scotland.

There is also, at the heart of her private life, a great tragedy. She was on the verge of a career as a concert pianist and was coerced into giving it up. A talent wasted on the altar of 'not the done thing'. And she was always haunted by the children she and the duke could never have.

She was never an MI6 agent, but the final judgement must be that she was an asset. There was nothing wrong with this by her own lights: she would have viewed it as further service to her country. It was not her fault that at this period the organisation was badly managed and penetrated at the highest level by a traitor. However, she was probably too naive to become involved in the world of spies, too ready to believe dubious Ukrainians with sanitised CVs, too ready to shake hands with her enemy's enemy, too in thrall to the likes of John Finlay Stewart, too ready to ignore uncomfortable facts if they did not fit in with her current moral crusade, and too lacking in the detailed background knowledge needed to unravel the complexities of middle and eastern Europe and make sound judgements.

Nowhere was her naivety more glaringly obvious than in the case of Dr Vladislav Dering. She died in 1960, coincidentally the year he returned to the UK, where he was finally to face his accusers in court.

Chapter Ten

Nemesis

During the 1950s the Nazi's genocidal campaign against the Jews made virtually no impact on popular culture in Britain. Only two books dealing with the subject made it into the bestseller list, *The Diary of Anne Frank* and Lord Russell's *The Scourge of the Swastika*. The latter, written in a sensational journalistic style, concentrated, however, on atrocities against prisoners of war and those committed against civilians in western Europe. Of the death camps, as opposed to slave labour and concentration camps, it covered Chelmo and Treblinka in a page and a half, and made no mention of Belzec, Sobibor and Majdanek. This generation of Britons did not really understanding the enormity of the decision reached at Wannsee to proceed with industrialised killing where human beings were detrained at one end and emerged as ashes at the other end of the process.

In 1959 Leon Uris published his blockbuster novel, *Exodus*. Although part of the novel deals with the final solution, its main theme was the foundation of the state of Israel. In the UK the main impact of the novel was its portrayal of Britain's duplicity in Palestine and of the Jewish guerrillas as [noble] freedom fighters in conflict with a repressive colonial administration backed up by a ruthless British army. The right-wing press condemned the book as 'anti-British'.

185

In 1962 Dr Dering's stepdaughter, Teresa Swifciki, read *Exodus*. On page 155 she reached a description of a medical block in Auschwitz: 'Here in Block X, Dr Wirthe used women as guinea pigs and Dr Schumann sterilised by castration and Clauburg removed ovaries and Dr Dehring performed seventeen thousand experiments in surgery without anaesthetic.'

She was outraged. She showed her stepfather the paragraph and told him he had to do something about it. He went to see his solicitor straight away. Many were later to wonder why he did not simply let things lie. In 1960 he had returned from Somaliland, received an MBE for his work in the colonial service, and set up a practice in partnership with an old friend from medical school, Dr Jan Gajek, in Seven Sisters Road. How many people in comfortable Ealing would have equated the misspelt Dehring in a single reference in an overlong novel with their own GP? Like many other war criminals, he could simply have merged into the background. Instead, he launched a libel suit against Uris and his publishers. One suspects that he saw himself as an establishment figure, invulnerable to being brought to task for events that seemed to have happened in the far-off other country of the Third Reich where they did things so very differently.

In April 1962 a letter from Dering's solicitor landed on the desk of the publisher, William Kimber, in New York. He called for substantial damages and an apology in open court. It caused some consternation when Uris revealed he had not done any original research on events in the medical blocks at Auschwitz, but had relied on information he had taken from a book called *Underground* by Joseph Tenenbaum. This was one of the earliest accounts of the Holocaust and was based on largely unsourced eyewitness accounts. To compound matters further, the publisher's lawyers discovered that Tenenbaum was dead; his widow had no idea of the sources her husband had used and had kept none of his notes. They handed over the case to Soloman Kaufman, a corporate lawyer of international standing.

Kaufman picked his English QC with care. He instructed Gerald Gardiner, Lord Gardiner of Kittisford, a future Lord Chancellor and one of the sharpest legal minds in England. Tall, thin, pale and austere, he used no histrionic tricks, but rather spoke with quiet effect, a master of the art of under-statement. He always stood ramrod straight and looked directly at the person he was addressing. It disconcerted hostile witnesses under cross-examination, reassured the friendly, and gave the impression to members of a jury that he was speaking Kitchener-like, directly to each individual. When required, he could, without affectation, descend from the lofty mode and use colloquialisms, in this case 'hoicking out ovaries', or 'that was anti-Semitism, that was'. Above all, in this case, he would be more than an advocate, however brilliant, arguing his brief and collecting his fee. There was emotional commitment. Gardiner had been the first British officer into Belsen Concentration Camp, a turning point in his life.

They got their first break through the Wiener Library in London, which specialised in twentieth-century Jewish his-tory. The library had a substantial dossier of clippings on the 1947/48 extradition attempt. The Jewish Refugee Organisa-tion had done their own research at the time and handed over a fat file containing the first trace of witnesses who had actually been operated on by Dering. The Israeli press took up the story and a journalist working on a book on Auschwitz contacted Kaufman with the names and addresses of victims he had interviewed. Through the Jewish community in Greece they traced two female survivors, one in Salonika, the other in the USA.

Meantime, the Wiener Library found Dering's name in a document drawn up for use in prosecuting Dr Carl Clauberg. Clauberg had been imprisoned by the Soviet Union in 1945, but handed over to the West German Federal authorities ten years later. After complaints from survivors he was held during criminal investigations, and died while awaiting trial in 1957. His dossier contained details not only of Clauberg's experiments, but also Dr Horst Schumann's in irradiating sex organs – and of Dering's part in extracting ovaries and testicles.

They found that the surgical register for Auschwitz had survived and was in the camp museum. With that curious Nazi passion for neatly recording even the incriminating evidence of the unthinkable, the record had been kept meticulously, first by Dering himself, then by an unknown hand. As the Red Army approached it had been smuggled out of Auschwitz by the camp underground before the Nazis could destroy it. The Poles were reluctant at first to release the records, but the combination of Gardiner's forensic logic and urbane charm, and Kaufman's no-nonsense New World common sense convinced them that they should co-operate. Dr Adelaine Hautval, who had refused to participate in the experiments, was at first reluctant to give evidence, but was eventually persuaded to do so by the formidable legal team.

They almost came unstuck over what might have seemed a simple problem: finding expert witnesses in the UK. They came up against the brick wall that was, and sometimes still is,

188

the self-protecting old boy and girl network of the medical profession. Senior physicians and surgeons would not testify against a fellow doctor. So Gardiner activated another network of the old school variety, and eventually a group of liberal-minded doctors were found through a personal friend of the solicitor.

Kaufman rented a flat overlooking Regent's Park and the lawyers assessed the evidence. They decided that they would have to admit that Dehring, with an 'h', was indeed the plaintiff. They could prove that Dering had performed 130 experimental operations, but the book claimed that he had performed 17,000. Kaufman decided to make an offer to settle out of court, based on their inability to substantiate the numbers involved, and to remove the offending paragraph from future editions of *Exodus*. The one thing Leon Uris would under no circumstances do was apologise.

Dering refused the offer. In March 1964, as part of the arcane working of the legal system, the publisher lodged forty shillings with the High Court and a trial date was set for 12 April. The judge was Mr Justice Lawton, Sir Fredrick Horace Lawton. As a linguist he could understand evidence in Hebrew, and 'the gist' of evidence in Judeo-Spanish; he also actually assisted in translations from the French. Dering's legal team was led by Peter Colin Duncan, whom Lawton described as 'the Homer of that section of the English bar concerning itself with libel'. In many respects he was the antithesis of his opponent, Gerald Gardiner. Duncan was short and spoke rapidly, the words 'almost tumbling over one another'. He did not look intensely at witness or jury, but addressed the court as a whole, looking to right and to left, or even behind counsel's row.

It would be an exaggeration to say that the Dering trial marked a turning point in British attitudes towards the Holocaust, but it was one part of a sea-change in attitudes. After the lack of interest of the 1950s, the new decade saw an increasing proliferation of memoirs, books, novels, poetry, plays and films dealing with the Nazi extermination programme and the concentration camps. A new generation was beginning to stare in horrified fascination at one of the darkest events in European history. Perhaps that is what Dering misjudged after more than ten years away from the UK. This was not the war-weary world of 1948, but 1964, where old easy assumptions were being questioned and challenged. On all eighteen days of the trial the public and press benches were crammed, and all available standing room filled.

The trial acquired a daily ritual of its own, a small dramatic moment which always silenced the courtroom. Each morning of the trial a courier brought the Auschwitz surgical register from the Polish Embassy, and each evening at the end of the proceedings it was returned.

The jury were sworn in. There were ten men and two women. They were middle-aged, so it is a fair assumption that most, if not all, the men had served in the Second World War, and, this being London, that the women would have experienced the horrors of bombing. The judge told them that he regarded it as his duty not only to assist them in matters of law, but to help them appreciate the dilemma of a 'professional man caught up in the hell of Auschwitz'. He posed a frightening question for them to ask themselves: 'How would I have come through this ordeal?' The question hung for a time in the stillness of a silenced court. 'I am relieved,' Lawton said to the jury, 'that it is you and not myself who has to judge the moral issues of blame or no blame.'

Many of the survivors gave their evidence anonymously. The 'First Woman' spoke in Hebrew through an interpreter. She had been born in 1925 in Salonika, and taken to Auschwitz in 1943. Lord Gardiner asked if she remembered her prison number. She nodded and drew up the left sleeve of her tweed coat, exposing her forearm. She could not find the words to actually tell the court the number, and bent her arm for the interpreter to see. He read out, '40574'. Her prisoner number was checked against the surgical register to confirm that she had, indeed, been one of the people operated on by Dering.

She said that the SS brought her, and nine other girls, to a place where 'I saw a big machine. They put two plates – there was electricity – one on my abdomen, one on the back. The effect of the machine was that the spot was dark and coloured and I vomited. The effects lasted about four weeks. Afterwards they called us again. They took us. We had a bath. Afterwards they sent us to a place opposite Block X; that was Block 21. Two men came and gave me an injection in the spinal column. Because of the pain I shouted, screamed and they took me to another room, put me on a table. There was a kind of screen before my face. There was a big lamp. I saw the reflections in the lamp. I felt they were doing something, but did not realise what.'

After the operation she was taken on a stretcher to Block X, where she was joined by the other nine girls as the day wore on. That night one of their number, Bella, died. The 'First Woman's' operation wound remained open for several days. Gardiner asked her about life after liberation. She had gone to

Israel, where she had married. In his quiet, even voice Gardiner asked, 'Have you any children?'

There was a long silence, and then she said, with a terrible finality, 'No.' The single word with its burden of sorrow resonated around the courtroom. People wept.

The 'Second Woman', whose number was 38762, corroborated the evidence of the irradiation, the spinal injection and the operation. She too remembered the girl called Bella who had died in the night. She also remembered Marta, who had been operated on twice, and Buena, who 'screamed very much and was taken out of the room and I never saw her again'. Above all she remembered their wounds, open for a week, with 'some dirt coming out', festering for all of two months, covered with bandages that were only paper, and a stench such that 'no one could stay in front of us because it was so unpleasant'.

The 'First Man' was called. Now thirty-eight and an Israeli citizen, he had been at high school in Salonika when the SS came in 1943. He was examined not by Lord Gardiner but by his junior, David Hirst. He asked the 'First Man' for his camp number. His hand shook and he struggled with his cuff links. Eventually he exposed the tattoo. The interpreter read out the figures: '114302'.

The 'First Man' told the court that after two days at Auschwitz he had been taken with some other young men to a room which was part of the women's camp. A Luftwaffe officer with a scar had been in charge, a man he later came to know as Dr Schumann. 'They told me I should put my genital organ, together with the scrotum, on a machine.'

There had been the soft sound of some kind of motor, and he had stood there, with this engine gently humming, for more than five minutes. When they had all been irradiated they were taken to Block 12 in Auschwitz. After some days they were moved and, with another man in the group, he had been taken into a doctor's room. Hirst asked the 'First Man', 'Who was present?'

'Dr Dering.' He pointed at the plaintiff. 'THIS Dr Dering.' The doctor remained impassive. 'At that time I did not know his name, but I now recognise him. Dr Schumann was also there.'

'Was anything done?'

'They told both of us to take off our clothes. Afterwards they gave us a piece of glass. Dr Dering came with a sort of club and put it into my rectum.'

Dering's lawyer, Peter Duncan, was on his feet. 'I object, My Lord. This piece of evidence has not been pleaded nor put to Dr Dering.' The objection was overruled.

Hirst continued, 'What happened after you were given the glass?'

'When he introduced the stick into my rectum, some drops came out of my member.'

'Who is "he"?'

'Dr Dering.'

The 'First Man' claimed that before his operation he had had a conversation with Dering and asked him, 'Why are you operating on me? I am fit, not sick.'

The doctor had replied, in French, 'If I don't take the testicle off you, they will take it off me.'

White-gowned male nurses had taken the 'First Man' to the operating theatre and held him down on one of two tables in the room. They tried to give him a spinal injection. He struggled and the needle broke. They cursed him in Polish.

After the second, successful, attempt he had 'terrible pains' and the lower half of his body went dead. He remained conscious.

'They took off the shirt I had,' he told the court, 'and put iodine on the skin, the left side of the lower abdomen. I was lying back. I saw the doctor putting iodine on with a swab. After some minutes I saw Dr Dering when he had my testicle in his hand and showed it to Dr Schumann.'

He later said that at this point Dering and Schumann had been 'very friendly and smiling'.

The defence brought in a succession of witnesses testifying to 130 operations carried out by Dering as part of the experimental sterilisation programme. Their harrowing evidence and the horrors that had been visited upon them made the task of cross-examination all but impossible for Dering's hapless legal team, led by Peter Duncan. He could only suggest at times that perhaps there was some confusion over some detail involving his client. Even an apparently harmless question could have hugely unexpected consequences. One woman who was still in the witness box when the court adjourned at the end of the seventh day returned next morning and said she would like to add something to her evidence. This concerned details about two girls, Marta, who had been operated on twice, and Bella, who had died after her operation. Thus far this middle-aged woman had been a calm and solid witness and had given her answers in a clear and composed voice.

Then Duncan rose to cross examine: 'Now about the time when you went to Block 21, in November 1943 . . .'

She burst into uncontrolled sobbing, covered her face with her hands and put her head down on the table. The judge spoke to the interpreter: 'Explain to the witness that she can go out for a few minutes.'

She was helped from her seat and walked down the steps from the court, supporting herself on the oak-panelled walls. She halted. The sobbing stopped. She turned her face to the wall, her arms outstretched in silent grief. The interpreter took her by the arm and led her out.

'My Lord,' Duncan said to the judge, 'I do not propose to subject the woman who has left to further cross-examination.'

In law, the defendants in the case were the author and his publisher, but as the tales of horror were unrolled, in moral terms it was the plaintiff Dering who was, in effect, turned into defendant. The 'Third Man' described not someone who was forced by terrible circumstances into being the unwilling tool of the Nazis, but a man who shared the Nazi world-view. The 'Third Man' had had first his right and then his left testicle removed, the latter by Dering. When he was on the operating table he had asked the doctor, 'Why do you operate on me? Is it not enough that they operate on me once?' and he answered, 'Dog, in any case you will die.'

The judge asked him, 'In what language did he speak those words?'

'In Polish.'

Gardiner asked the 'Third Man' to say the words in Polish.

'Przestan szczekac jac pies, tak i tak umrzesz.'

The Polish interpreter translated the words as: 'Stop barking like a dog. You will die anyway.'

Dering's junior counsel, Thomas Neill, rose to his feet. 'Are you sure that these words were not used on some other occasion by a German?'

'No.' The 'Third Man' spoke quietly. 'Only HE said it.'

'Are you saying that you can remember the exact words twenty years later?'

'Yes.'

The judge asked the witness to repeat the words and directed they should be put in writing, shown to Dering, and entered as an exhibit.

Gardiner re-examined: 'Were you Polish?'

'I was a Jew.'

'How long had your family been Polish citizens?'

'For generations.'

'Did you expect to be spoken to like that by a Polish doctor?'

The 'Third Man' answered in Hebrew. The interpreter translated: 'He had always spoken in a rude manner. He was an anti-Semite.'

The judge asked the jury to put the last remark out of their minds. It is doubtful, with the best will in the world, if they could.

The medical evidence was damning. William Nixon, Professor of Obstetrics and Gynaecology at London University, who had practised surgery for forty years, had examined eight of the women victims. He told the court: 'I have practised in China, Africa and the Middle East, and I have never seen such scars as I saw last week, such scarring, such deficiency, such pigmentation.'

Only one voice was raised in Dering's favour from the Auschwitz survivors. Dr Jan Grabczynski had been sent to Auschwitz in 1942, and said that from 'my own observation Dr Dering had treated his patients well and looked after them properly'. This was in the camp hospital, before the orders for experimental operations in Block X. He was asked by Peter

Duncan, Dering's counsel, if he remembered Dr Schumann requiring these operations to be carried out.

'Yes.'

'Was there a discussion among the prisoner doctors about these operations being carried out?'

'Yes.'

'Did you personally receive any instructions from Dr Schumann?'

'Personally, no. But Dr Dering told us he had received an order from Dr Schumann.'

'Tell us what, after these discussions, the doctors decided to do?'

The answer from Grabczynski was disingenuous in the extreme: 'As Dr Schumann had given the explicit order that these operations were to be performed, it would have fallen to the SS corporal or nurse to perform them. The doctors were of the opinion that, for the sake of those who were to be operated on, it would be much less risk if they were operated on by doctors.' This was disingenuous because it gave the impression of a unanimous decision. Only he himself and Dering agreed to carry out the operations. Three remarkable women doctors defied the SS.

The first of these to give evidence was Dr Doroto Lorska, aged about fifty, dark haired, with a pleasant round face that belied the horrors she had seen and suffered. She was wearing a no-nonsense blue and black tweed suit when she took the stand. She was of Jewish extraction and had volunteered as a doctor on the Republican side during the Spanish Civil War, where she had become a committed Communist. When the Civil War ended she went to France. After the German occupation her husband had vanished into what the Nazis

197

called Nacht und Nebel – night and fog – an instrument of terror where people simply disappeared into the concentration camp system. She joined the Resistance and after the war was awarded the Croix de Guerre by General de Gaulle. In 1943 she had been arrested by the Vichy police, handed over to the Gestapo and sent to Auschwitz. 'A German SS doctor, Wirthe,' she said, 'after events which were worse than Dante's hell, turned to us and asked which of us were married women. Before I had time to reply he noticed on my sleeve a band with a red cross. He asked me if I was a doctor. I said, 'Yes.' Then he made me join a group of about sixty women who declared themselves to be married. That is how I got into Block X.'

When she arrived she met one of the other remarkable women doctors, Adelaine Hautval, who told her the purpose of the block: that the Nazis were performing experiments on Jewish prisoners. 'The Germans,' Dr Hautval had said, 'will not allow people to know what is going on here. So the only thing that is left to us is to behave, for the short time that remains to us, as human beings.'

The judge asked Dr Lorska: 'If Clauberg – who was an SS general, was he not? – had said to you, "Tomorrow morning you will take that girl's ovary out'," I gather you would have refused?'

'I think I would rather have committed suicide.'

'What would have happened if you had simply refused?'

'I would have been given some heavy duties.'

'Nothing more than that?'

'I don't think so.'

In the case of Dr Hautval the question was not a hypothetical one. She had refused to do operations involving the sterilisation programme on four occasions. She had been summoned by Wirth and she had told him, 'You can send me up the chimney. I will do no operations involving experiments on human beings.' She then found herself appointed as assistant to a German doctor carrying out experiments on Jewish twins and had again refused. The doctor had simply shrugged his shoulders and said, 'If she won't she won't.'

The other female doctor was, of course, Alina Brewda. Petite and middle-aged, she now lived in London. She gave her evidence in a calm, matter-of-fact manner. She had first met Dering when she was a student. They were 'quite friendly', and they met from time to time at the Polish Students' Association. He had married a fellow student, Krystyna Ossowka, some time after 1930. In September 1940 Brewda had been sent to the Warsaw Ghetto, where she lived until the rising in 1943. She was sent to Majdanek concentration camp and then to Auschwitz. In Block X she had examined all the women and found that about 150 of them were being used in sterility experiments by Wirth and Clauberg, who injected caustic fluid into the womb. They were all Jewish.

She spoke Polish, Russian and French and so managed to communicate with most of the women who had been experimented upon. The French were the youngest, 'really only children'. They were 'terribly afraid of grown-up persons', their most recent experiences of adults having been the visitations of SS doctors who regarded them as sub-human subjects for experimentation. She had tried to contact Dering and, after a second message, he had met her in the corridor of Block X. When he appeared he 'was, as always, smartly dressed in a good suit and clean shaven'. Dr Brewda had asked him for milk for the girls. He said it was 'quite impossible'. She asked for white bread. He offered her some for herself, which she refused. The only role she accepted was 'to comfort the patients'. Asked by the judge if she would have performed an operation she said she would have refused.

The truth is that by 1943 the disasters on the Eastern Front meant that the Nazis were facing a desperate shortage of doctors and concentration camp authorities had been ordered to save medical staff. As Gerald Gardiner put it in his final statement: 'The Auschwitz hospital was not there for the benefit of the prisoners. It was there for the benefit of the Germans, who needed able-bodied people as slave labour, and it was sense if you had a septic thumb or leg to have a place where it could be put right.' In the awful logic of the system, if an illness or ailment was going to take longer than six weeks to cure then it was deemed more cost-effective to send the prisoner to the gas chamber. Nevertheless, if a doctor refused to work on experiments then he or she was still needed to feed the slave labour machine that was the working part of Auschwitz.

Dering appeared on the stand twice. At the beginning of the trial he had argued that he had no choice: do the operations or die. He tried to argue that after August 1943, when he was no longer writing up the surgical register himself, the ink looked fresher and may have been tampered with. Yet, even in this opening appearance, he could not deny that he had, in fact, taken part in experimental surgery, although he did try to muddy the waters of truth. 'They were not', Gardiner asked him, 'operations being performed for medical reasons, were they?'

'It depends. It could be done in normal circumstances.'

The judge was not impressed, 'Well, Dr Dering,' he asked, 'who wanted these operations performed, Dr Schumann or the patient?'

'Dr Schumann.' Dering answered the question flatly, without emotion.

Gardiner returned to the attack in his quiet level voice: 'And you knew that Dr Schumann wanted them for his experiments?'

'Yes.'

'If you knew Dr Schumann wanted them for his experiments they were experimental operations were they not?'

'The experiments had been done before, by X-ray. That was the first step; if you like it was the second step of his experiments.'

'And therefore it was an experimental operation?'

'In this way, yes.'

'Were they all young Jews?'

'Yes.'

At the end of Dering's first appearance the judge told him to take the Auschwitz surgical register in his hands, to stand up so that everyone could see him, and to open it at random between the beginning and a point which had been flagged by the court. He should then read out the English equivalents of the entries, to demonstrate a typical day's work in the operating theatre. Dering opened it at page 112. He read out a catalogue of minor operations. His voice faltered as he read the final entries, operations he had carried out to remove the testicles of three men as part of the experimental programme, recorded in his own handwriting.

When he took the stand the second time, towards the end of the trial, the evidence of his victims had been heard, the three women doctors had demolished his argument that he had had no choice, and the odium of anti-Semitism clung to him. Suddenly there were things he could not remember.

Gardiner introduced the testimony of the 'Third Man', who had asked the 'perfectly reasonable question' why he had been operated on twice.

'But I don't remember this kind of talk and especially his sentence in Polish.'

'You said, "Stop barking like a dog. You are going to die anyway."'

'Lord Gardiner, any Slavonic language specialist will tell you that this kind of sentence could not be said by any Pole. It is not according to the spirit of the Polish language. It is not a Polish sentence.'

Gardiner raised the eyebrow sardonic. 'This man was a fellow Pole – but it was not a Polish sentence.'

Yet this was not the trial of Dr Dering for war crimes; it was a libel trial, and he had not, in the offending words, 'carried out 17,000 experimental operations'. Even Brewda had withdrawn the allegation and told the court she no longer believed that it was as many as that, though this was the number Dering had boasted of performing. That was an odious boast, and the remarkable thing, from the doctor's point of view, was that the trial he had instigated had mired his name far more effectively than the single misspelt paragraph in *Exodus*.

The judge's summing-up lasted five hours and he opened by reminding the jury that: 'We are not here acting as a war-crimes tribunal, nor are we conducting an inquiry about what went on in Auschwitz. We are here to try a civil case according to the law of England.' He reminded them that their test was what 'an ordinary level-headed average citizen' who knew Dering, or knew of him, would think the paragraph meant. 'Up to the point of the trial,' the judge said, 'The average reader of *Exodus* would have little or no idea who ran the camp. Many people where Dering practised or where he lived might have taken this book out of the library and read this passage without connecting it with Dr Dering in any way. It could not mean anything to them unless they connected the name "Dehring" with the name "Dering" and knew that Dr Dering had been in Auschwitz.'

The jury took two and a half hours to reach its verdict. At almost half past two on that bright May afternoon the jury-room bell buzzed in court. They filed back into the two narrow benches and the usher asked who was the foreman. A large middle-aged man in the centre of the front row stood up and said, 'I am.'

'Are you agreed on your verdict?'

'We are.'

'Do you find for the plaintiff or for the defendants?'

Absolute silence fell on the packed court.

'For the plaintiff.'

'What sum do you award the plaintiff against the defendants?'

'One ha'penny.'

There was a communal gasp in the courtroom and sudden movement in the press box.

'And that is the verdict of you all?'

'Yes.'

The judge executed something of a coup de grâce. Mr Justice Lawton ordered Dering to pay the costs of the defendants after the date of the payment of forty shillings by the publishers in March. This meant that the doctor was faced with paying the full legal costs of the trial, in excess of £20,000, an enormous sum in 1964.

Outside in the May sunshine the swinging sixties were being born, the beehived dolly-birds in ever-rising hemlines were clicking their high-heeled way down the Kings Road; Mick Jagger and Marianne Faithfull were supping in the World's End pub; 'Bedlam in Edinburgh', 'Frenzy in Glasgow' the headlines screamed of the Beatles' tour, the latest James Bond, *Goldfinger*, had just been released. A *Daily Express* reporter sought out Dering's partner. Dr Jan Gajek told him: 'It is easy for people here in Britain in 1964, comfortable and well fed, to sit in judgement on how things were in Auschwitz twenty years ago. It was a different world. Only those who were there know what it was like, the death rate, the brutality. It is nonsense to say he was a monster.'

Dering was ruined. Pursued by threatening mail, he vanished into the obscurity of poverty. His wife told reporters: 'We won, but it does not seem to have got us very far.' Did Gajek's jibe have substance; did we judge horrors of which we knew nothing? Perhaps. But, as Gardiner pointed out, Dering never expressed remorse; in all these terrible operations on young men and women there was not one act of compassion, not one single kind word. Even in the witness box he never once expressed regret.

Chapter Eleven

Conclusions

The twin engines of this story have been the two pseudo-religions of the twentieth century, Nazism and Soviet Communism. In the 1930s the United Kingdom armed and paid ethnic resistance movements within the Soviet Union and eastern Europe, movements which were also taking money from the Nazi secret service. Most of these organisations were of a far-right, racist and anti-Semitic hue, and when Nazi Germany attacked the USSR, they threw their lot in with their soulmates in Berlin.

They helped prolong the war. By 1945 a generation of young Germans had been decimated, sacrificed on the altar of National Socialism in battles waged on fronts from the sands of North Africa to the snows at the gates of Moscow, perishing in the steel coffins of U-boats in the grey North Atlantic or burning to death in aircraft in clear blue skies above the English countryside. The greatest killing ground of all was the vast Eastern Front.

The poet Gottfried Benn, a doctor, was an early supporter of the Nazis who rapidly became disillusioned. In late 1944 he was working at a barracks and noted that the new recruits for the East were, 'sixteen-year-olds, underfed, scared, submissive, and the old codgers, aged fifty to sixty, from Berlin'. The training period was short – less than a month – and they were taking target practice on the second day, something which came only after six weeks in the old Wehrmacht training regime. 'Then, one night,' Benn wrote, 'they line up with full pack, almost a hundred pounds of weight, and off they go to be shipped out, into darkness. New ones come in the morning. They also leave. The barrack blocks stand, the waves roll. New waves of blood due to trickle into the eastern steppe after a few shots.' Younger, fitter blood came from the legions raised amongst Stalin's disaffected, the peoples who had no wish to be part of Lenin's 'Great Experiment', until, by the war's end, one in eight of Hitler's soldiers was a citizen of the USSR.

The success of the Nazis in recruiting Soviet citizens was a beguiling precedent when the West faced the expansion of Stalin's empire into eastern Europe. Hitler's quip when he invaded the Soviet Union, that 'one kick on the stable door and the whole rotten edifice will come crashing down', proved to be misguided, and he mismanaged relationships with the disaffected ethnic minorities. Yet the remark was based on a reality. The USSR was not a homogenous whole: it consisted of disparate nations and peoples, many of whom not only loathed Stalin and Communism, but held a deep and lasting hatred for the whole notion of Russian rule. They had that often distorted sense of great historic wrong which belongs to the small people oppressed by the bigger neighbour. To the nationalists of the Ukraine, the Baltic and the Asian Soviet Socialist Republics, the commissars and the secret policemen were but the latest manifestations of Moscow rule, and Joseph Stalin just another Tsar, albeit a particularly brutal and nasty one.

Conclusions

At first sight, Western exploitation of this scenario would seem to have been an unmitigated, and often almost farcical, endeavour: a steady stream of agents dropped behind the lines, a steady stream of failure, betrayed by Kim Philby, or penetrated at the local level by Soviet Intelligence. In many cases it was counter productive, and the operations were used to send back disinformation. Such an analysis, however, is too simplistic. It fails to take account of the paranoiac nature of Stalin and his regime. The show trials of the late 1930s, the purging of senior party figures, able officials and, above all, officers in the Red Army depleted talent within the apparatus of the Soviet state, and brought near-catastrophe in 1941 when the Nazis invaded and all but overwhelmed a poorly-led opponent.

When Yugoslavia broke with the Soviet bloc in 1948 and Tito gave the world a non-Soviet version of Communism, he provoked Stalin's paranoia into a wave of repression and purges throughout his empire. Beginning in Albania in the spring of 1949, these purges were widespread and far-reaching. Stalin's personal paranoia was not merely metaphorical, it was clinical. Khrushchev once overheard him mutter, 'It is finished, I trust no one. Not even myself.' Support for ethnic nationalism by Western Intelligence served to feed his disturbed state of mind, driving on his orgy of arrests, show trials and executions in eastern Europe, and often destroying the ablest and the best minds with his eternal hatred of intellectuals and of the successful. There were high-profile scalps – the Hungarian Foreign Secretary, Laszlo Rajk, the Bulgarian Deputy Premier, Traicho Kostov and Otto Sling of the Central Committee of the Czech Party to name but three – but there were literally

hundreds of officials purged, usually from ministries of Foreign Trade or Foreign Affairs.

Stalin had a particular fear of the machinations of MI6, believing it to be a dangerous and devious enemy, a view he saw as justified by their subversive activities in the Baltic and the Ukraine. Given the state of the service in the late 1940s and early 1950s this may seem like further proof of a deranged mind out of touch with reality, but there was another quite rational reason for specific Soviet fear of Britain. It was, quite simply, the challenge represented to the Marxist-Leninist world vision by Western European social democracy in general, and the Labour government in London in particular. As Elma Dangerfield in one of her editorials in the *Whitehall News* in 1945 put it: 'The trend in Europe is towards the left, but overwhelmingly towards the democratic left. The choice is not now between Russia and the plutocratic West, much more it is between Russia and democracy.' As the Attlee government powered ahead with a social revolution, the creation of a National Health Service and a Welfare State, the ideological and propaganda war intensified.

In 1948 the Russia Committee noted that the Soviet Union was 'increasingly hostile to Britain, as well as to the political and social ideals which this country shares with other Western democracies', and that recent Soviet publicity had launched 'an increasingly vehement offensive against Western Socialism and its leaders in different countries'. The Soviet Union played on a number of themes designed to appeal to the left of the Labour Party, most notably its traditional anti-Americanism. A typical example appeared in the magazine *Trud*. An article in December 1947 claimed that: 'Together with British monopolists the Labour leaders are paving the path for American Imperialism which is striving for world domination.'

However, Soviet propaganda hit home harder when it attacked the somewhat grim domestic situation in the UK. For all the government's radical changes, Britain in 1948 was far from being the New Jerusalem. There were shortages, rationing and austerity. Moscow Radio ran a series of 'first-hand impressions' of Soviet citizens who had, they alleged, visited Britain. A Soviet teacher from Vladivostok claimed: 'The parents of many British school children are familiar with the words Black List. Entered in that list are more than 600 schools considered unfit for studies.' A 'Soviet Seaman's Impressions of Hull' were grim indeed: 'Half-naked, dirty children are picking out the refuse bins on a street corner.' One D. Mospanov claimed to have visited Glasgow, where he stayed at a hotel called The Railwayman. He found a 'terrible food situation', largely involving breakfasts of inedible kippers and porridge. On his journey north there was no food on the train and he was 'saved from starvation by a fellow traveller who had brought tins of jam, sugar and other things'. He had little time for British Rail: 'For six hours I looked out of the window of my carriage and saw our train overtaken by cars, motor cycles and bicyclists; even a good runner could have passed us.'

More important than the propaganda, which was more often than not too heavy-handed, was the actual subversion practised by Soviet Intelligence in Britain and Western Europe. The discredited over-reaction of the McCarthy witch-hunts in the United States allowed many on the left in Britain to dismiss out of hand the reality of Kremlin-backed espionage as 'reds under the bed' hysteria. We now know from sources which have been opened up throughout the old Eastern bloc that there really was a fifty-year-long conspiracy to foster political and social unrest in western Europe by the KGB and its sister services.

In the early 1980s the doyen of experts on NATO and the Eastern Bloc, the late John Erickson, Professor of Defence Studies at Edinburgh University, claimed that the institution was 'riddled with spies'. The general reaction of the Scottish press corps – and I include myself in this – was that he 'had lost the plot'. We were wrong. Exposure of the KGB files in the Mitrokhin archives revealed that an Edinburgh student and academic, Robin Pearson, had been recruited by the Stasi, the East German secret service, in 1978. Further research by Professor Anthony Glees in the Stasi files has unearthed a wealth of detail on just how far students and lecturers were targeted for recruitment, identified as propaganda assets, or simply spied on because they were hostile to Communism.

In Christmas week 1980 senior Stasi officers held a series of meetings with their Scottish spy ring in Inverness and in Skye. Amongst those identified by Pearson was, bizarrely, Graham Watson, then deputy secretary of the Young Scottish Liberals. He was approached in 1986 when he worked for the former Liberal leader David Steel at Westminster. Watson, of course, rejected the attempt at recruitment. He went on to become a LibDem MEP, and believes the government should consider prosecuting the alleged traitors.

The Soviet Union itself was in some difficulty in trying to make capital out of the student radicalism of the 1960s and '70s. The brutal and very widely reported suppression of the Hungarian rising of 1957 and of the 1968 Prague Spring made a huge dent in support for the Communist Party and in lingering working-class and intellectual sympathy for the USSR. This was why recruitment for the likes of the Edinburgh University ring was made through the secret services of a satellite state rather than by the KGB itself. It was still possible to believe perversely that if Moscow had lost its way, things were different in the other so-called people's democracies.

In Europe the Cold War was a covert war. This does not, however, mean that it only took place up dark alleys in East Berlin where the plans of nuclear submarines were passed to fedora-hatted agents, or in grim Prague hotels where honey traps were set for diplomats, or in the tense few minutes it took for a spy to come in from the cold through Checkpoint Charlie. It could also have more domestic British settings. The Scottish League for European Freedom was, on the surface, a charity. Many people worked hard for that charity, collecting clothes for refugees, raising money, sending food parcels, visiting refugee camps, all believing that what they were doing was helping people who had been dispossessed. In fact they were, more often than not, unwittingly helping war criminals. They were deceived, and it is in the nature of covert warfare to deceive innocents.

It is also in the nature of covert warfare to create strange alliances. The nationalism fostered by MI6 within the Soviet Union was of an ethnic kind which easily tuned in with Nazi ideology. The conclusion of the Foreign Office research department in 1948, that breaking up the USSR on ethnic lines would 'put the clock back 400 years', turned out to be not far short of the mark. In 1991, with the writing already on the wall, Mikhail Gorbachev said that 'Communism is the cement that holds the Soviet Union together'. He was right. The break-up of the union, however, did not lead to the creation of liberal democracies guided by the rule of law. There was no deep well of democratic tradition to draw from, no sense of civic nationalism, only ethnic division and tribalism. In the old Asian Soviet Socialist Republics the long-suppressed dogmas of Islam have returned. In Russia itself there is a continuing tradition: that of the secret police. Vladimir Putin is an old KGB hand and the KGB is an organisation with an unbroken thread that runs back to the instruments of Tsarist repression, a tradition of control and terror where only the acronyms have been changed. Russia is a democracy, but not as we know it. It sometimes seems as if authoritarian Russia stands on the brink of an awesome new horror: Stalinism without the ideology.

This story is rooted in the 1920s and 1930s when John Finlay Stewart was meeting Bandera and Stetzko in the forests of the Soviet borderland. What drove Stewart? Like many spies he was in love with the thing itself, but he was also driven by hatred – hatred of the Russians. It was the great age of hate. Your political predilections came with pre-packed scapegoats, be they kulaks or Jews.

In the period between the First and Second World Wars it seemed as if the values of western liberal democracy were lost, and that the future lay in either Berlin or Moscow, or even with the corporate fascism of Mussolini. Of course, economic failure was a major factor. In 1929 Weimar Germany was enjoying a degree of prosperity, laying the foundations of a welfare state, and by 1930 it had overtaken Britain as the second-largest exporting nation. The Nazi threat seemed stalled. This was swept away by the storm of the Great

Depression. Yet the fascination of totalitarianism is not explained by economics alone.

'A new era of magical explanation of the world is arising' is an interesting text, which could have come from the lips of any number of visionaries of the left or the right, or even from the lips of a tree-hugging New Age hippy. In fact it came from the lips of Adolf Hitler. 'There is,' he said, 'no truth either in the moral or the scientific sense.' This is the language of faith.

The Soviet Union made much of its pretence to be a scientific society, but it was just that – a pretence. For more than thirty years its agricultural policy was based on the delusions of Trofim Lysenko. He held that bourgeois genetics had an unacceptable philosophical base, and that the science should be based on the sounder principles of dialectical materialism. Lysenko married the official state philosophy to the theory of acquired characteristics, a long-discredited notion which flew in the face of scientific evidence. He convinced Stalin that by using his 'science' new strains of winter wheat could be developed. Stalin died before Lysenko's failures came home to roost, but, undeterred, in 1954, he went on to convince Khrushchev that exotic crops like corn could grow in Siberia. Khrushchev was, at the time, launching his Virgin Lands programme, which opened up new arable farming in Khazakstan and western Siberia. The 'new' biology chimed in perfectly with Khrushchev's dreams. No winter wheat grew in Khazakstan, no corn on the cob ripened in Siberia. It was an act of faith, as unscientific as the Inquisition denying the motion of the planets round the sun.

The virtues of Western liberal democracy are oft trumpeted – freedom of speech, the rule of law, free elections – but underpinning the virtues is a bedrock: the pursuit of objective truth. It is one of the great discoveries of the West. It is something derided by post-modernists and by cultural relativists. They deride it at their peril. As the geneticist Richard Dawkins put it: 'Show me a cultural relativist at 30,000 feet and I will show you a hypocrite. Airplanes built according to scientific principles work. They stay aloft, and they get you to your destination. Airplanes built to tribal or mythological specifications, such as the dummy planes of the cargo cults in jungle clearings or the beeswaxed wings of Icarus, don't.'

The story told in this book is intimately intertwined with the threats that emerged from two societies which embraced two appalling and murderous faiths: Soviet Communism and German Nazism. It raises two huge questions. The first is how do you combat such a threat? Both sought to use propaganda and subversion to destroy democracy and to impose an inhuman world-view on mankind. Unless you are a pacifist it seems clear you have to accept that these could only have been countered by propaganda and by using the black arts of espionage and spying.

Once you have entered the secret world you enter the world of moral ambiguity, of making alliances with your enemy's enemy which will lead you-know-not-where, of fine distinctions between freedom-fighter and terrorist, between being the assassin and merely paying for the assassination. Once you have entered such a world the ideals of democracy and open accountability can, at best, only be extremely limited. Bureaucracies left at such arm's length will have a tendency to develop their own policies and world-view. The best to be hoped for was to contain the worst excesses of over-enthusiastic spies whose detachment from the real world was so great that they devised hopeless and dangerous adventures. The idea that an ethical espionage policy in countering the Nazi and Soviet threat could have been developed is a delusion.

The other huge question is why millions of people were in thrall to Hitler and Stalin and their ideologies. When Stalin died, hundreds were trampled to death in the weeping crowds converging to mourn outside the Kremlin. German widows sent Hitler gifts and Russian widows sent Stalin gifts; families built domestic shrines to the dictators; when they passed, people tried to touch them as if they were endowed with thaumaturgic power; the girls of the League of German Maidens held parties where they saluted and screamed 'Heil Hitler' until they achieved a literally orgasmic climax; on Stalin's fiftieth birthday in 1929, 'clouds of incense wafted towards Moscow from every town, village, factory and barracks in the land'. It was a demonic world from which reason had fled.

Tamerlaine, who celebrated victories with pyramids of skulls, would have understood Stalin perfectly, only envying the twentieth-century despot his command of technologies that could provide death measured in the millions rather than in the hundreds or thousands. The Third Reich killed more Jews in four years than the Christian church managed in four centuries because it could harness the power of industrialisation and mechanised transport. Spanish inquisitors, Aztec priests, Praetorian guards, witchfinder generals, Chinese emperors – all would have felt at home in Stalin's Russia or Hitler's Germany.

Perhaps these represent the norm of human history, and the comforts and decencies of liberal democracy are destined to be destroyed by the beast of faith within us. After all, even today, when the values of the West are supposed to be in the

215

ascendent, transported by the alleged benefits of globalisation and an international media, most human beings are still enslaved by authoritarianism, tribalism, theocracy or superstition. If that all sounds like a counsel of despair, that's because it is.

Bibliography

Unpublished Sources

The bulk of the material for this book came from the papers of the Foreign Office, the War Office, the security services and the Cabinet Office held at the Public Record Office in Kew.

Newspapers and Periodicals

ABN Correspondence
Daily Express
Daily Mail
Daily Telegraph
Edinburgh Evening Despatch
Glasgow Herald
Lobster
Manchester Guardian
The Nineteenth Century and After
Perthshire Constitutional
Scotsman
Searchlight
Sunday Times

Tribune
Whitehall News

Pamphlets

The pamphlets and publications of the Scottish league for European Freedom are in the National Library of Scotland and the Public Record Office in Edinburgh. Those of the British League for European Freedom are in the British Library.

Printed Books

Aarons, Mark & John Loftus (1991), *Ratlines: How the Vatican's Nazi Networks Betrayed Western Intelligence to the Soviets*, Heinemann
Aldrich, Richard J. (2002), *The Hidden Hand: Britain, America and Cold War Secret Intelligence*, Overlook Press
All Party Parliamentary War Crimes Group (1988), *Report on the Entry of Nazi War Criminals*
Andrew, Christopher & Vasili Mitrokhin (1999), *The Mitrokhin Archive*, Allen Lane
Annan, Noel (1995), *Changing Enemies: The Defeat and Regeneration of Germany*, HarperCollins
Arms, Thomas & Eileen Riley (1994), *Encylopedia of the Cold War*, Facts on File
Ascherson, Neal (1987), *The Struggles for Poland*, Michael Joseph
Atholl, Katherine, Duchess of (1938), *Searchlight on Spain*, Penguin
————— (1958), *Working Partnership*, Arthur Barker
Benn, Gottfried (1950), *Doppelleben*, Limes Verlag
Bethell, Nicholas (1987), *The Last Secret*, Coronet
Boelke, Willi (1966), *Kriegspropaganda, 1939–1945*, Deutsche Verlaganstalt
Borovik, Genrikh & Philip Knightley (1994), *The Philby Files: The Secret Life of the Master Spy*, Little Brown
Bower, Tom (1981), *Blind Eye to Murder: Britian, America and the Purging of Nazi Germany – A Pledge Betrayed*, Deutsch

Bibliography

————— (1987), *The Paperclip Conspiracy: The Hunt for Nazi Scientists*, Little Brown

————— (1989), *The Red Web*, Aurum Press

Bullock, Alan, with Peter Hennessy & Brian Brivati (eds.) (2002), *Ernest Bevin*, Politico's Publishing

Calvocoressi, Peter (1947), *Nuremburg*, Chatto & Windus

Cave Brown, A. (1988), *'C': The Secret Life of Sir Stewart Graham Menzies, Spymaster to Winston Churchill*, Macmillan

Cecil, R. (1988), *A Divided Life: A Biography of Donald MacLean*, Bodley Head

Cesarani, David (1992), *Justice Delayed: How Britain Became a Refuge for Nazi War Criminals*, Mandarin

Charmley, J. (1995), *Churchill's Grand Alliance: The Anglo–American Special Relationship, 1940–57*, Hodder & Stoughton

Conquest, Robert (1991), *Stalin, Breaker of Nations*, Viking

Churchill, W.S. (1951), *Speeches*, Cassell

Dangerfield, Elma (1993), *Beyond the Urals*, T. Lyster

Dickens, Arthur (1947), *Lübeck Diary*, Gollancz

Dorril, Stephen (2001), *MI6: Fifty Years of Special Operations*, Fourth Estate

Fabian Society (1945), *Population and People*

Fuller, Major General J.F.C. (1936), *Memoirs of an Unconventional Soldier*, Nicholson and Watson

Gilbert, M. (1976), *Winston S. Churchill, 1922–39, vol. 5*, Heinemann

Glees, Anthony (1987), *The Secrets of the Service: British Intelligence and Communist Subversion, 1939–51*, Jonathan Cape

————— (2003), *The Stasi Files: East Germany's Secret Operations Against Britain*, Free Press

Goebbels, Joseph (1987), *Die Tagebücher*, Institut für Zeitgeschichte

Griffiths, Richard (1983), *Fellow Travellers of the Right: British Enthusiasts for Nazi Germany, 1933–39*, Oxford University Press

————— (1998), *Patriotism Perverted*, Constable & Robinson

Hill, Mavis (1965), *Auschwitz in England: A Record of a Libel Action*, MacGibbon & Kee

Ingrams, Richard (1995), *Muggeridge: The Biography*, HarperCollins

Jenkins, Roy, Lord (2002), *Churchill: A Biography*, Pan

Judd, Alan (1999), *The Quest for C: Mansfield Cumming and the Founding of the Secret Service*, HarperCollins

Knightley, Philip (1989), *Master Spy: The Story of Kim Philby*, Alfred A. Knopf

Kulski, Julian (1979), *Dying, We Live*, Holt, Reinhart & Winston
Le Quex, William (1908), *Spies of the Kaiser*, Hurst and Blackett
Loftus, John (1982), *The Belarus Secret*, Alfred A. Knopf
Macleod, Douglas (1995), 'Germany Calling Scotland', *Journal for the Study of British Culture*, Tübingen University
———— (1982), Interview with James W.D. Anderson
———— (1981), Interview with Julian Rybarczyk
Magnusson, Magnus (1967), *The Glorious Privilege*, Nelson
Muggeridge, Malcolm (1973), *Chronicles of Wasted Times* (2 vols.), Collins
———— (1981), *Like it Was: Diaries*, ed. J. Bright Holmes, HarperCollins
———— (1934), *Winter in Moscow*, Eerdmans
PEP (1948), *Population Policy in Great Britain*
Philby, Kim (1969), *My Silent War*, Grafton Books
Rosenberg, Alfred (1943), *Blut und Ehre* Zentralverlag der NSDAP
———— (1944), *Deutsche und Europaische Geistesfreiheit*, Zentralverlag der NSDAP
———— (1934), *Der Mythus des 20 Jahrhunderts*, Zentralverlag der NSDAP
Seth, Ronald (1952), *A Spy Has No Friends*, Deutsch
———— (1939), *Baltic Corner*, Methuen
Tannahill, J.A. (1958), *European Voluntary Workers in Britain*, Manchester University Press
Voigt, F.A. (1938), *Unto Caesar*, Constable
West, Nigel (1992), *Secret War: the Story of SOE, Britain's Wartime Sabotage Organisation*, Hodder & Stoughton

Index

Note that names beginning 'Mac' and 'Mc' are indexed as spelt.

221

Bandera, Stefan 68–9, 159
  CIA and MI6 dissension
    over 156, 160
  flees west 139–40
  and Fuller 90–1
  and MI6 163
  and Stewart 127
  terror campaign in camps
    143
  Ukrainian SS Division 138
Barbarossa 69
Barnes, Major 33–4
Battle of the Ghetto 19
Baykolov, Anatole 116–18
BBC 48, 59
Belarus Legion 150
Beneš, Edvard 99, 100
Benn, Gottfried 106, 205–6
Bennett, Sir Ernest 50
Bergmanis, August 105
Beria, Laurenti Pavlovich
    123
Berling, General Zygmunt 17
Berzins, Alfreds 150
Bevin, Ernest
  on Communism 78
  and Ukrainian SS Division
    128
  on war criminals 174, 175
Blackett, Frances 116, 121–2,
    171, 172
BLEF see British League for
    European Freedom
Bletchley Park 65
Blitzkrieg 62, 89
Blunt, Anthony 158, 160
Boer War 27–8, 85–6
Boothby, Robert 53
Borovik, Genrikh 158
Bower, Tom 92, 93, 94, 122
Bradford cathedral,
    monument to former SS
    166
Brewda, Alina 171–2, 176,
    178, 199–200, 202
Britanova 12, 13, 116
British Broadcasting
    Corporation see BBC
British Empire Union 91
British League for European
    Freedom (BLEF) 2
  and anti-Polish feeling 139
  and Baykolov 117–18
  decline 182

and Dering 171, 172, 177,
    178
  founding by Kittie Murray
    81, 84
  and Latvia 119
  pro-Balt lobby 114–16
  and Soviet slave colonies
    119
British Union of Fascists
    (BUF) 49, 54
Brocklehurst, Philip 57
Brody, Battle of 130
Brooke, Field Marshal Sir
    Alan 76, 77
BUF see British Union of
    Fascists
Burgess, Guy 158, 160
Burns, Tom 116

Cairncross, John 158
Cakars, Maris 143
Calvokoressi, Peter 180
Cambrai, Battle of 89
Canterbury, Archbishop of
    137
Carlyle Club 50
Carlyle, Thomas 50
Carr, Harry 92, 104, 125,
    145, 156
Cavendish, Anthony 122
Celtic nationalism, and Nazis
    52, 53
Celts 50, 51, 52
Central European Federal
    Study Clubs 70, 80, 97
Cesarani, David 166, 180
Christie, Malcolm 117
Chuprynka, Taras 140, 159
Churchill, Sir Winston
  1945 election defeat 78
  assumes power 62
  and Baykolov, Anatole
    117
  correspondence intercepted
    60
  Danubian Federation 70
  denazification trials 180–1
  faces deselection 53, 56–7
  Hapsburg Empire recreated
    66, 70
  and Kitty Murray 55–6
  Operation Unthinkable
    74–6
  Poland 71

Special Operations
    Executive (SOE) 65
  and Stalin 75–6
  Yalta Conference 71
CIA (Criminal Intelligence
    Agency)
  Albania 147
  Baltic operations 125
  European Movement 181–
    2
  Safehaven 104
  Ukraine 143, 145, 146
Clauberg, Carl 169, 170,
    188
Clay, General Lucius D. 140
Cohn, Norman 102
Cold War 211
Coleridge-Taylor, Samuel 24
Common Cause 182
Communist Party (in Soviet
    Union), Jewish nature of
    Central Committee 48
Communist Party of Great
    Britain 182
  and Kitty Murray 81–2
  loss of support for 211
  conscription, and SNP 53
Conservative Party
  Kitty Murray fights by-
    election as independent
    55–6
  and Munich Agreement 53
Convention of Resistance
    Movements (Edinburgh)
    1–2, 149–50, 152, 153,
    154–5
Cooper, Sir Alfred Duff 3,
    53
Cossacks 109
Coudenhove-Kalergi, Count
    66
Crail 155
Cripps, Stafford 110
CROWCASS (Central
    Registry of War
    Criminals and Security
    Suspects) 120, 168–9
Crowley, Aleister 37, 89
cultural relativism 214
Cyrankiewicz, Jozef 178
Czechoslovakia 53, 99–100

Dangerfield, Elma 2–3
  British League for

Index

Morningside Mata Haris

Index

Lviv 69, 91, 127
Lysenko, Trofim 213

MacCormick, John 53
MacDiarmid, Hugh 50–1
Mackenzie, Compton 51
Mackie, Marjorie (cover
  name Marjorie Amor)
  57
MacLean, Donald 158
Maclean, Sir Fitzroy 129–30,
  131
Maisky, Ivan 40
Major, John 163
Malta 147
Manchester Guardian
  Muggeridge in USSR 36,
  37, 38
  Voigt's reporting on
  Weimar Germany 10, 12
Manstein, Fritz Erich von
  180
Marcus, Karl 101
Martowych, Oleh 142, 144
Matthias, Ludwig 60
Matwijejko, Mynon 159,
  160
McKibben, Alexander
  'Sandy' 104
McKibben, Sandy 93
McLean, Neil 148, 151, 152,
  163
McNeil, Hector 131–2
Mein Kampf 40
Memoirs of a Revolutionary
  35
Menzies, Sir Stewart 65, 67,
  77, 91
Meyer, Sir Anthony 178
MI5
  and Anna Wolkoff 61, 63
  and Dering 170–1, 173
MI6 (Secret Intelligence
  Service, SIS) 13
  Albania 147–9
  Anti-Bolshevik Bloc of
  Nations (ABN) 70
  in Baltic States 92–3, 94,
  104–5, 123–6
  and Burns, Tom 116
  Convention of Resistance
  Movements meeting
  (1950) 2, 151
  and Dangerfield, Elma 20

and Dering 173
and Durcansky, Ferdinand
  98–9
émigré operations ended
  165
establishment 163–5
and Fuller 90
funding of operations 103–
  4
and Gehlen 101
Hapsburg Empire recreated
  66
Intermarium 67, 78–9
and Kitty Murray 82, 184
Middle Zone Association
  80
and Neil McLean 151
Operation Jungle 124
OUN 68, 90–1
Philby, Kim 156–9
Promethean League 67,
  68
recruitment of 'Nazis'
  100–1
and Slokenbergs 98
SOE 65
Soviet Union 77–8
Stalin's fear of 208
and Stokes, Richard 115
Ukraine 140, 144–6, 156
Ukrainian SS recruits 155–
  6
and Voigt 12, 20
Westward Ho scheme 114
MI9 3
Middle Zone Association 20,
  80, 114
Miller, Joan 57, 61
Modin, Yuri 160, 162
Molotov 9
Moncrieff, Sir David 92
Montgomery, Field Marshall
  Sir Bernard 72, 140
Moore, Sir Thomas 91
Moscow Radio, propaganda
  against Britain 209
Mosley, Sir Oswald 49, 57
  MI5 views on 63
Muggeridge, Malcolm 36–8,
  60
Mulhausen, Professor
  Ludwig 52
Munich Agreement 53
Murray, Katherine *see*

Atholl, Katherine
  Duchess of
Musketeers 148
MVD-MGB 143

Nacht und Nebel 198
Nachtigall 68, 69
Narvik raid 63
National Citizens Union 42
Nazis
  in Baltic States 93–4
  disposal of assets post-War
  103
  genocide, impact of in
  Britain 185
  largest gathering since
  Nuremberg 149
  recruitment of Soviet
  citizens 206
  and Scotland 50–3
Nazism
  in East and Central Europe
  101–2
  and Fabians 111–12
Neill, Thomas 195
New British Broadcasting
  Station 52, 59
*Nineteenth Century and
  After, The* 9, 148
Nixon, William 196
NKVD 15, 141, 142
Nordic League 49, 88
Nouvelles Equippes
  Internationales 181
Nuremberg Rally 51
Nuremburg Trials 7, 180

Office of Policy Coordination
  141
Officers and Gentlemen 51
Ohio, Operation 143–4
O'Malley, Owen 6, 7, 70–1
Oras, Ants 96, 104
Organisation of Ukrainian
  Nationalists *see* OUN
Orwell, George
  on anti-Polish sentiments
  139
  British League for
  European Freedom
  (BLEF) 114–15
  censorship of anti-Russian
  writings 14
  on Kitty Murray 43

Index